Books by Jacqueline Hornor Plumez

Divorcing a Corporation:
How to Know When—and If—a
Job Change Is Right for You

Successful Adoption:
A Guide to Finding a Child and
Raising a Family

DIVORCING A CORPORATION

DIVORCING A CORPORATION

How to Know When —and If— a Job Change Is Right for You

Jacqueline Hornor Plumez, Ph.D.
with
Karla Dougherty

Villard Books
New York
1986

LIBRARY OF CONGRESS CATALOGING IN PUBLICATION DATA
Plumez, Jacqueline Hornor.
Divorcing a corporation.
Bibliography: p.
1. Career changes.   2. Job hunting.   3. Vocational guidance.
I. Dougherty, Karla.   II. Title.
HF5384.P58   1986   650.1′4   85-40183
ISBN 0-394-54457-9

Manufactured in the United States of America
9   8   7   6   5   4   3   2
First Edition
Designed by Beth Tondreau

To my family,
for giving me love and support

and to U.N.T.,
for giving me inspiration and tenacity

Note to Readers

For years I have been asking people personal questions about their work. I have been trying to find answers to questions that nagged at me. Questions like: Why is it so hard to leave a job, even a job you hate? Why do good people get stalled along the career path? And when is it right to stay with a company even if you are offered a "better" opportunity? Almost everyone I approached was willing, and often even eager, to talk about these subjects . . . subjects that confused and troubled them, too.

Once people started talking, they quickly got into their feelings about their own jobs. When assured of anonymity, they openly explored the private reasons they felt attached to their companies, and their fears about their careers. Many said they had never discussed these things with anyone before. If I needed proof of how secret these subjects are, I had only to listen to the few spouses who sat in on interviews. They usually remarked, "I never knew you felt like that."

I am thankful to my interviewees for being so open and frank. I was especially gratified by a number of highly revealing talks with personnel experts who work for major corporations.

To maintain privacy and job security, I identify my subjects with false first names and occasionally with altered job titles. The quotes, however, are real. On the other hand, I am happy to quote by name some of the executive recruiters, employment agency owners, and consultants who generously gave me their time and their thoughts.

In *Divorcing a Corporation* I have tried to map the emotional iceberg of career planning. I have tried to provide practical methods of coping with the 90 percent that is hidden beneath the surface of any stay-or-leave job decision.

I want to continue my research, so I am asking you to share your experiences with me. If after reading this book you successfully divorce your corporation *or* stay and find a way to work out a better relationship, please write and tell me how you did it. I would like to include many of these letters (anonymously or not) in a sequel to this book, and I will appreciate your help.

Jacqueline Hornor Plumez, Ph.D.

Contents

Introduction

Family Secrets

"Everybody wants to belong to something,"
—Personnel manager,
Fortune 500 company

"The company is a place where you belong."

That is what a seasoned editor told me during our first interview. "When I took a leave of absence for a year, they kept my mailbox. But one day I came back for a visit and my mailbox was gone. I almost cried. It wasn't a status thing. It really meant I didn't belong there anymore."

Another executive, someone who worked for IBM, referred to his firm as "Mother IBM"—without any prompting from me.

Delta Airlines' in-house slogan is "Family Feeling," permeating every department from traffic to sales.

In fact, almost everyone I interviewed, regardless of his or her company's slogan, felt at some level like the woman who said, "My office feels like home."

And home is where the heart is.

Family feeling. Belonging. Home. I've heard these phrases over and over again during the three years I've researched this book. Whether the people I interviewed loved their jobs or hated them, whether they were secretaries or senior vice-presidents, whether they felt stuck or felt satisfied—it made no difference. Consciously or without even realizing it, they talked about their company in familial terms.

It makes sense. We spend more time on the job than we do with our real families. It provides a constant in a world where 50 percent of our marriages end in divorce, where 50 percent of us move to a new community every five years.

We might not recognize a soul on our way to the supermarket, but every morning the office receptionist greets us with a big smile and friendly hello. We might not know all our neighbors, but we can gossip with our friends at work about everyone from the chairman of the board to the crazy secretary in Purchasing. The office is a secure base, financially and emotionally. At work we have our in jokes, our stories, and our daily dramas. Our real families can't possibly understand our world at work. They can listen. They can offer advice and be sympathetic. But they don't live it.

SKELETONS IN THE CLOSET

Quite simply, we are what we do—and where we do it. As much as we try to have interests, goals, and life-styles separate from our careers, our jobs are enmeshed in the friendships we make, the places we live, the way we dress—and even the way we think.

With this kind of impact, it is vital that we feel good about our corporate home—and many people do. They've found their niche in a challenging, supportive corporate family and, wisely, refuse to be lured away by any headhunter's siren call.

But for every happy member of the corporate family tree, there are many who are not. In fact, executive recruiters estimate that four out of every five Americans are dissatisfied with their jobs. Yet even the unhappiest employees often refuse offers that could change their lives. Why? What are these ties that bind us to a corporate family for better or for worse? Why do so many people continue to stay in jobs they hate? Why do they get stuck?

It was these continuing questions that gave me the incentive to write this book. Because it is tough to leave a corporate home and family—even the homes we hate.

I know. Not only because I've spent the last fourteen years as a practicing psychologist and career counselor, not only because I've interviewed over one hundred corporate beginners, managers, vice-presidents, executive recruiters, and personnel experts around the country, but because I've lived it.

The first year I was married, I had to coax my husband out of bed every morning to go to an engineering job he hated at Mobil. After two unhappy years, he decided on a career switch and was accepted for his M.B.A. at Wharton. Instead of feeling happy, he was miserable. As the time approached to quit his job, he became more and more nervous and irritable. Even though he disliked his work, it represented a huge personal investment. It was hard for him to turn his back on all the time and energy he'd spent. He was afraid that he was running away from a challenge —and admitting defeat to the world that included a father who always wanted him to be an engineer. He almost backed out to stay at Mobil for a secure, but self-destructive, career. Though no one ever knew it, he went through hell.

Happily, his fear eventually faded as he plunged into his classes, and he was graduated with top honors. Today he is a successful advertising executive. But it took a lot of courage and —equally important—a change of attitude: he discovered he had the power to move on.

Years later, when my daughter was born, it was my turn. I was a staff psychologist at a mental health center. It was only a part-time job. The commute was bad, the pay was lousy, and I didn't like the bureaucracy. There was no question that I wanted to leave to enjoy motherhood and to explore new career opportunities. But I couldn't quit. I took a six-month maternity leave instead, writing and rewriting my letter of resignation during those six months, and throwing each letter away before I finally sent one.

I am a self-confident and independent woman, but just like my husband, I felt insecure when it came to leaving my job. Instead of a clean break, I clung to the shreds of belonging, purpose, and identity the clinic provided. My steady paycheck took on a worth far in excess of its size. Although I had my Ph.D. from Columbia University, I was afraid that without an organization behind me, I would no longer be a psychologist; I would become "just" a wife and mother.

Making that final split was one of the most difficult things I have ever done. The period between letting go and feeling re-established was a rough one, but exhilarating too. I finally had the courage to divert my energies into building a successful private practice and writing career.

Through personal experience, I learned that leaving a job is not leaving "just a job." In actuality, it's getting a divorce. It's as wrenching an experience as marital divorce, with the same kinds of change in routine, identity, financial state, social life, and life-style. You're forced to face the same unpleasant process of saying good-bye and finding another niche in the vast unknown. And as with marital trauma, many of us are tempted to turn our heads, staying on in an unhealthy situation that can hurt our chances for the future.

Right now, eighty million Americans are at least toying with the idea of changing their jobs. And up to twenty million will probably go through the process this year alone, many leaving when the best career move might be to stay put. I don't want them to have to go through what my husband and I went through—and what thousands of others have gone through—unnecessarily.

Divorce is extreme, and it is smart to try to work things out before you make that final break. But you *don't* have to stay in the wrong corporate family 'til death do you part.

A STRESS IN THE FAMILY

It's not enough to work hard. It's not enough to follow all the rules. It's not even enough to understand the politics. The key to a successful career is knowing when to stay in a job—and when it's time to make a change.

But change—any change—is stressful, and our natural inclination is to avoid it whenever we can. In fact, research psychologists have found that some of the most stress-producing situations in life involve changes on the job.

It's easy to understand why getting fired or receiving a pay cut or living through a business merger made the top of the list. What is surprising is that these negatives shared the same space with the stress produced from *positive* change. Changes such as getting a promotion or a raise were found to cause as much stress as getting a demotion or a pay cut. This angst is compounded by the fact that most people expect to feel good, not anxious, when they make a change for the better. They don't talk about their anxiety for fear of sounding irrational or emotional, something that goes against the sane, unruffled, in-charge corporate image.

Although one manager I know disliked his boss and didn't think twice about accepting a job offer that doubled his salary, he found himself racing for the Valium bottle in the two weeks before starting this better job. A colleague of mine was promoted to an important position at a metropolitan hospital. She had a migraine headache for weeks even though she was excited about the new job. Another friend, "the golden boy" of a major bank, had been passed over for promotion. When he was offered a better job somewhere else, he accepted happily, thinking, "Boy Wonder Sticks Finger in Eye of Large Commercial Bank." His satisfaction soon turned to anxiety, and for the next ten days he had terrible bouts of nausea. He dreamed he was fired from his new job and his children were walking around with tiny, bloated stomachs, hopelessly starving.

Peter Grimm, co-owner of executive search firms in New York

and Chicago, calls this "gangplank fever," a phenomenon recruiters see all the time. They give candidates fantastic job offers. The candidates seem really excited. But at the last moment the candidates change their minds. Filled with worry, they back out. As Grimm says, "It's more comfortable sleeping with dragons you know than with ones you don't."

Recruiters chalk this behavior up to fear of change and the unknown, but I've discovered it's *much* more complicated than that. In *Divorcing a Corporation* I will deal with all the hidden ties that bind us to an unsatisfactory job.

A GOOD FIT

It is important to remember that we are not always tied to a job with unhealthy rope. There are many valid reasons for staying in a job that have nothing to do with stress, fear, or misguided family loyalty:

The field feels right. If the lure is money and high finance, you'll look to commercial banks, financial houses, or the stock exchange. If your interests lie in the arts, you'll find your niche in publishing or in a gallery or in the entertainment industry. The reasons why you stay on the job once you get your feet wet are as different as the initial lure for every field. These reasons often change as you begin to understand your industry's ins and outs. Government employees, for example, often go into their line of work because they want to do something worthwhile and meaningful. If they come up against bureaucracies and daily roadblocks that thwart their need to do good, the security of the job —its excellent benefits and pension plans—can become the reason for staying.

The position feels right. Like water, we all seek our own level within our chosen field. For short-term comfort, the position must provide the right mix of challenge and security. For long-term comfort, it must clearly point us to the ultimate rung to which we aspire along the career ladder. And speaking of the ultimate rung, some people want to rise to the top ranks of power, while others know they'll be more comfortable settling in somewhere along the way.

The benefits feel right. Each level within a field has its own lure that may or may not keep you satisfied. Whether it be security or prestige, short hours or creativity, mental stimulation or upward mobility, all of us will find the unique reasons to stay where we are. I've identified over forty psychological and financial benefits different companies provide that tap into our values, needs, and aspirations—and I'll help you find your best combination later.

The particular firm feels right. Each company has its own culture, its own reasons and regulations for doing things. If your firm's personality is compatible with your own, you'll enjoy your stay—and have a home for life.

The boss's supervision feels right. If your boss is a good teacher and helps open doors to new opportunities, you'll want to stay —at least until you've learned everything you can. Your career— and even your health—can benefit. Research shows that workers who receive emotional support from their bosses are physically healthier than their colleagues who have unsupportive ones.

YOU feel right. From the field you enjoy to the boss who delegates, from the benefits that lure you to the challenge of the work, if all elements are simpatico, there's no reason why you should leave. But sometimes even the best-laid plans go astray and a good fit can get tight. It can happen overnight, with new management directives, or slowly, over a few months, as you notice that your projects are getting turned down, your supervisor is no longer seeking you out. . . .

Even a great job can turn bad. It's hard to face when it happens, but it's even harder to know what to do. Here are some typical situations that many of us, at one time or another, have fallen into:

GETTING ULCERS INSTEAD OF GETTING OUT

You like what you do, but you hate where you're doing it. Maybe you have a boss who constantly criticizes you, refusing to recognize your good work. Or maybe you're being ground down by incredibly long hours, and there's no time to think about finding another job. You've lost touch with your old contacts. Your skills have gotten too specialized, too geared to your company's way of doing things. Whatever it is, you're not happy . . . and it's getting to you.

TOO LOYAL TO LOOK AROUND

You like your boss and you know you're needed. But your career's not progressing fast enough. Maybe you're earning less money than your friends and colleagues in similar jobs in different companies. Maybe you sense you're in a dead-end job. Or maybe sales have dropped and there's talk of cutting back. Your ship is sinking—or stalled in the water. And you're too loyal to even think of jumping off.

FIDDLING WHILE A CAREER BURNS

Once upon a time you were the fair-haired child of the place. You could do no wrong. But suddenly you've been losing a client here, an account there. People aren't coming to you for business advice the way they once did. You haven't solved anything more difficult than a crossword puzzle in the last few months. Something *is* wrong, but you can't seem to write that résumé.

"IS THAT ALL THERE IS?"

Peggy Lee asks this in a song—and you may be asking it too about your job. You're not exactly miserable. But you're not happy, either. You like your job. Sort of. Maybe you need a vacation. It just doesn't seem bad enough to actually go out and *do* something. . . .

Introduction

WEARING SNEAKERS IN A WORLD OF SHOES
It's you. Everyone else is walking around the office brisk, efficient, in control. They like chatting about the politics at the water cooler. They like writing memos. They like sales conferences. They like the abstract paintings displayed in their offices. But you don't. You're bored. Frustrated. Going to work is a chore. Instead of thinking that maybe this corporation isn't for you, you try to fit the square peg into the round hole. And you don't dare talk about your feelings with anyone. . . .

No one intentionally gets stuck in a world of shoes with his sneakers untied. You don't get stuck in a job you hate on purpose. But many people get so locked into their organizations that they never check to see if they could do better. They stay and peak before they should. As one manager at a Fortune 100 company asked: "Why didn't they leave when they should have? Are they lazy? Are they scared? Did they talk themselves into something that wasn't right? I've seen so many people get stuck in jobs making fifty percent less than they could. They start making excuses. They start feeling inertia. And inertia is the greatest asset a company has."

Still others develop the opposite problem. Instead of inertia, they're constantly on the move. Avoiding attachments, they hop from job to job never making the kind of commitment that is a prerequisite to success.

It's sometimes smart to leave; no one wants to fiddle while a career burns or sing a sad song along with Peggy Lee. On the other hand, it's sometimes smart to stay. Any job, even a bad one, gives us something good. Its emotional and financial benefits cannot be cavalierly thrown out like an old winter coat. Making the choice that's right for you can mean all the difference between a career that succeeds and one that doesn't.

TO GO OR NOT TO GO:
THAT IS THE QUESTION

The answer is a high-stakes decision that needs cool, calm, rational thought. Unfortunately, it's a complex choice fraught with emotion and confusion. Even M.B.A.s who make tough, logical business decisions in the workplace every day often can't make rational decisions about their own careers. I've talked to people known for their brilliant corporate strategies who couldn't begin to figure out how to improve their current situation—or how to look for a new one. They felt frustrated, but even their close friends didn't know. People are not accustomed to expressing their fears in the business world—even if they could find a supportive, safe, knowledgeable ear.

Countless books line the shelves describing the logistics of job change. There are books on selecting a career, books on résumé writing, books on the how-tos of effective job campaigns. But before we can effectively put a plan into action, we have to recognize the underlying "whys." We have to understand all the powerful, often familial, attachments we find at work in order to use all that good, solid advice in the best way possible. Then, and only then, can we be free to choose: to stay, to look around, or to leave for a better home.

This book explains the invisible psychological corporate infrastructure so you'll be able to diagnose your own situation rationally and accurately. In the next few chapters I will analyze the hidden emotional aspects of your corporate family, starting with the early years when you're a child in the family circle with a boss-parent and a whole crew of siblings and, later, when you actually become wedded to a corporation and become a boss-parent yourself. Once you understand the family ties that bind, you'll be able to determine your own corporate blueprint and see for yourself if you're staying in your job for the right reasons or if you're trapped in an unhealthy home. You'll learn the ways smart managers differentiate job problems they should stay and overcome from ones that derail careers and turn good people into deadwood. You'll be able to build the confidence you'll need to "divorce" your corporation if need be—or stay on to change things for the better.

And in case it's really time to move on for your own personal growth, you'll have a step-by-step program to help you land on your feet, diminishing the stress—and risk—of change.

Corporate life should be stimulating and rewarding. You can earn a lot of money and be happy at the same time. The ideal can turn into reality.

It did for my husband and me. It did for many of the people I interviewed for this book. And it can for you.

You *can* love your work and find—or create—a healthy family environment in which to do it.

Part 1

THE CORPORATE FAMILY

Chapter 1

Be It Ever So Corporate, There's No Place Like Home

Home sweet home:
"I love my company. They are the family I turn to when I'm in trouble. They are the people I can confide in. It's hard work, but we have fun."　　　　　　—Production manager,
　　　　　　　　　　　　　　　　　　Fortune 500 company

Home sour home:
"As much as I hate my job and the people, I know I'd miss them if I left. I know what to expect and what I have to do."　　　　　　　—Another production manager,
　　　　　　　　　　　　　　　　　Fortune 500 company

"It's a real family."

"I keep thinking what a nice feeling to be with people I really enjoy being with. I enjoy going out to dinner with them. I enjoy playing tennis with them."

"What a feeling to walk in the bar after work and have everyone know you and have everyone say hi!"

"I don't really like all the people all that much, but there's a loyalty or security or something. I'd be lost without them."

These people are talking about their corporations, not their aunts or uncles and not the folks who live next door. The corpo-

3

ration has become the family of the 1980s, and the office has replaced the neighborhood.

When Freud once declared that the keys to mental health were love and work, he was talking to a completely different world, where work was something men did during the day while women stayed home to tend the hearth. Home was the fortress that kept chaos at bay. Work provided the financial means to keep it secure.

No more. Love and work are no longer two separate ideals. The corporation has taken up the void left by the shrinking family and the dissolving community. The corporation has become the new fortress in an unfriendly time, a stable entity in a confusing and changing world.

With more women working, and everyone spending longer hours on the job, the focus of our lives has changed from home to office. That makes the relationships we form at work more important than ever. For many people, office friendships are the best ones they have. Water coolers and coffee machines have become the gathering places that back fences used to be. When we want to see friends, we stroll down the office corridor—just the way our grandparents might have strolled along their small-town streets.

On a deeper level, it's hard to avoid reacting to our bosses as parent figures when they are doling out direction, protection, scoldings, and praise just like Mom and Dad used to do. The support we gain from our good friends at work can make us as close as brothers and sisters, and the competition for raises and recognition can bring out the worst of sibling rivalry. It is hard to leave a close and supportive family. But as every psychologist knows, it is even harder to break away from a bad one.

Bad or good, emotionally close or distant, our companies exert an enormous and growing influence on our lives. As the book *Corporate Cultures* states, corporations "provide structure and standards and a value system in which to operate."

Families used to do that.

Presidents and chief executives are beginning to realize that it is in their best interest to act like home and family to their employees. After all, top on the list of what makes a place one of the *100 Best Companies to Work for in America* is its ability to "make people feel that they are part of a team or, in some cases, a family."

Our corporations are consciously evoking feelings that are already in place, backing our natural tendencies with seductive policy. As a personnel manager at a large investment house told me, "Managers are encouraged to get to know their people on a personal level. Employees are encouraged to socialize together, to get close. We don't want them to leave. We want to make them feel if they went someplace else, they'd be leaving the family."

NOT ALL IN THE FAMILY

In a society where change is constant, the corporation where you work can easily become the most stable element in your life. All around the country I found strong corporate family feelings in the most unlikely people. Even businessmen who do not seem to have an emotional bone in their bodies become fervently attached to their companies, clinging to them like a lifeline.

In fact, many people are happily sacrificing their personal life for their corporate life—actively choosing their corporate families over their natural ones. For single people, the office often supplies the nourishment and a sense of belonging they don't get elsewhere. A client of mine, whom I will call Julie, quit her public relations job to write a novel. "Yet I'd go back and visit my department all the time. I didn't even like all those people that much. But it was home." In less than six months, Julie went back to work for the firm. "There was a great sense of relief when they told me I could come back. I needed the connection. I could go home knowing my old room wasn't rented out." Her novel, half-finished, sits in a desk drawer.

Neither does being married make you immune from the corporate family "tug." Jim and Susan are typical of the couples I met who seem more married to the corporation than to each other.

Both Jim and Susan are successful young professionals, dedicated and serious about their careers. They work long hours to stay ahead on the fast track. "There just doesn't seem time to make friends outside the office," said Susan. "The few neighbors I met and liked when we first bought our house moved away. I hardly even know the new ones."

Most evenings Jim and Susan have little time to sit and talk to each other. Each weekend they make plans to spend time alone together, but something usually comes up to distract them: paying the bills, chores around the house . . . or paperwork from the office. They're so wrapped up in their individual careers that domestic responsibilities feel like the real "work," while work itself—with its clear challenges and tangible rewards—is a stimulating game. They'd never admit it to each other, but more times than not, they'd rather be at the office than at home.

In the past, workaholics like Jim and Susan were scorned. There had to be something wrong with them. Not anymore. Recent research has shown that, as a group, workaholics are amazingly happy. They are working hard at what they love. They can't get enough. "Workaholic" no longer has the terrible connotation with which it was once saddled. Of course, there are those "Type A" workaholics on a treadmill, consumed with a bad habit that will eventually burn them out. But basically a workaholic is the quintessential "family man"—1980s corporate style. They don't suffer at all. Their *real* families often do.

Let's face it. Workaholic or not, the corporate family can be exciting and a lot sexier than most real families. Mates have a hard time competing with million-dollar deals. In an office, there are even more plot twists and turns and melodrama to keep you going than on the prime-time soaps. While half the country is sitting around watching high-rolling family intrigue on *Dynasty,* the other half is *living* it—at work. And what a cast of characters:

THE HEROES

These Movers & Shakers look right, talk right, and think right, and everyone learns something from watching them. Their business decisions benefit both their own careers and the long-term interests of the company. Juggling enormous pressures without getting riled is second nature to these heroes and heroines. Which young fast-tracker will become the Heir Apparent and which ones will start to sweat . . . losing their aura of invincibility? Tune in tomorrow to find out. Heroes at the top are brilliant and rule in several different ways:

1. *The Elder Statesmen* may delegate much of the running of the business to others while they assume highly visible roles in public affairs. Their outside activities lend an aura of high-minded elegance to the firm.

2. *The Patriarchs* are wise and powerful parental figures who create a corporate family image, kindly "fathers" and "mothers" who rule with a magnanimous hand.

3. *The Dealmakers* are the crème de la crème of negotiators and strategists. Everyone can rest assured that the company will grow and prosper with a Dealmaker actively steering the ship.

THE VILLAINS

Beware the Bad Seeds. Often only instinct warns you that these guys are bad. They have been known to move in on many a good Mover & Shaker unawares. They're out there ready to spring:

1. *The Gunslingers* like to come in and add some notches to their belts, then move on to a newer sunset. Found with a short-term profit mentality that makes the bottom line look great—at first.

2. *The Roman Emperors* instigate great unproductive political

wars. Not above backstabbing in the dark alleys of high company intrigue.

3. *The Crooked Politicians* are elegant sleaze-bags on the take. Somehow you know their sons' bar mitzvahs or daughters' church weddings were paid for by their suppliers—or a padded expense account.

DADDY'S GIRLS AND MOMMA'S BOYS

They are utterly loyal to their bosses because they think their "parents" are wonderful. Sincere ones can be abused or taken advantage of by manipulative bosses. Less sincere ones are manipulating themselves. They can be serious competition, especially if insecure leaders only want watered-down clones. . . .

THE LAZY UNCLE

This corporate relative spends more time dodging work than doing it. May once have started out ambitious, but his lights are dimming. More interested in getting to the bar after work or home to TV than in achievement. Will he be found out and dumped?

THE DIZZY AUNT

Always running into work late or into a meeting with papers flying. Repeatedly warned about tardiness or missed deadlines—to no avail. She always has a good excuse, and her stories are so good that even if people don't believe them, they let her talk. Not a serious competitor because she doesn't understand that work has to be the number one priority.

THE NEIGHBORHOOD GOSSIP

If you want the lowdown on anything from who's sleeping with whom, who's expected to get a raise and what they're going to get, just ask her (or him!). Nobody knows how gossips know what they know; possibly they possess superhuman hearing and an uncanny ability to read upside down. The gossip is sometimes used as a conduit when someone wants information to get around unofficially. Gossips are not serious contenders because they can't keep company secrets. . . .

Every corporation is a different family playing out a different drama, with the spotlight focused on the smart, aggressive Movers & Shakers. The sparks fly when they do battle against the outside competition, the inside villains, and sometimes even against themselves. But for comic relief and colorful distraction, there's a whole other cast of "character actors" in supporting roles, usually including your company's version of The Sexy Blonde, The Complainer, The Madonna, and The Nerd. You might not like them. You might have nothing in common with them. But somehow they *are* part of the family circle.

When you seriously consider divorcing a corporation, there's no doubt you will be upset about leaving your well-known role —or rut—in the unfolding family drama. You will feel conflicted about leaving your network of Mover & Shaker friends. But— believe it or not—you may even be nostalgic about leaving behind The Nerd.

FAMILY LIFE

Whatever role you play, the corporation eventually becomes intertwined with every facet of your life, from your child's college tuition loan to your annual medical checkup and everything in between:

1. Office episodes become shared history, the stuff of legends. How many times do we reminisce about "the night George got so drunk we had to drag him into a taxi while he was singing 'On the Road to Mandalay' . . ." or "the time the marketing plan was a mess and everyone pitched in to save it. We worked forty-eight hours straight to get it on the client's desk by nine A.M.—and he *loved* it."

9

2. *There's instant identification and prestige*. Think of the boost from saying "I'm with Xerox" instead of the drab, flat tones of "I sell office equipment."

3. *There are all the addictive financial and psychological benefits that feed our basic insecurities*. Our needs for approval, belonging, and money are met while, at the same time, thoughts such as "If I don't make it here, I'm a failure" and "Why look around? At least I know what I have here" often spring up.

Corporations *consciously* encourage these feelings. There are company picnics and company softball teams. When someone has a baby, everyone chips in for a gift. There are retirement parties, promotion celebrations, Christmas parties, farewell parties, welcome-back parties. . . .

The longer you stay in a job, the harder it is to leave. As a woman dating a young "Mother IBM" man explained: "He belongs to the company country club. He goes to the company picnics. It's a real family setup, and he needs that because he's shy and lacks confidence. He doesn't have to go out and make any effort. It's all planned. He can live his whole life within that structure."

With or without this corporate conditioning, almost everyone *unconsciously* begins to think of his or her company as home sooner or later. From top executives to secretaries, from the savvy Elder Statesman to the new kid on the block, from go-getter employees who love their jobs to drones who hate them, eventually emotional attachments sneak up.

This works well when both corporate and individual needs are satisfied. In the ideal family organization, everyone has a respected place. Each person fits in with the company culture. Lifestyles are compatible. Profits are up, work hums, and morale is high.

Even in the most supportive corporate families, however, we must be aware that we are not born into corporate structures; we are brought in to be productive. Overriding any family ties, there exists a business whose first priority is profit. If you lull yourself

10

into a false sense of family security, you can be in for a big surprise.

Consider the case of an executive I'll call Bill.

He went to work in a family-run firm where the president treated him just like a son. But the president had a *real* son, and when he decided to retire, he brought in his flesh and blood. Bill was devastated. He was sure the president would have wanted him to take over. After all, he was "family."

On a much larger scale, there's Exxon, a corporation that has taken pride in its career development program and lifetime employment. Exxon fostered the belief that when they hired you, they retired you. But during a recent financial downturn, the company fired hundreds of "family members." One manager told me: "Everyone was in total shock. People were walking around very depressed. They were like zombies."

Although these are two extreme examples, *every* person gets trapped in a job in a different way, and *every* corporation spins its unique web. It's vital to understand your family ties because the important career decisions you make throughout your life depend on it. Decisions can only be made in a rational way when you are aware of your hidden emotional attachments to your corporation.

Surprisingly, I've discovered that few people are fully aware of this family feeling in their corporate home, and even fewer know how it developed in the first place.

SETTLING IN

People merge with their corporations at different times, depending on individual needs and backgrounds. If your needs for security and belonging are strong when you start a new job, chances are you'll develop corporate family feelings much more quickly than someone who is driven more by power or achievement. And if your father or mother had set an example with long and fruitful family ties at work, you'll be likely to want the same. "My father worked twenty-five years for the same company, and if his firm hadn't moved, he'd still be there today," a young manager told me. "I just assumed I'd join my company and stay there forever."

Others let the commitment creep up. In fact, executive recruiters tell me that after eight to ten years, people become so tied to their corporate home that it's very hard to pry them loose —even for a new and better one.

And why not? Every relationship deepens with time. When you first start your job, you're the vulnerable "new kid on the block," dependent on others for guidance. Eventually you grow up and move into a position of authority yourself. Your relationship with your corporate family matures. Congratulations. Wedding bells are ringing, and you've unconsciously tied the knot.

MARRIAGE VOWS

In the 1950s, William Whyte, Jr.'s best-selling book, *The Organization Man,* took a look at the business world and the gents in the gray flannel suits, the men who believed, "If I'm loyal to the company, the company will be loyal to me." In order to climb the corporate ladder, you *had* to marry the corporation.

Then came the anticorporate '60s and the job-hopping '70s. Through it all, corporate marriage had its rewards. As the head of an executive search firm told me: "You can only become part of the top brass if you live, breathe, and think the company. The rest get stuck with the Peter Principle." Statistics bear him out: 50 percent of all current chief executive officers have been with their companies all their lives. In the new world of the pin-striped suit, the problem becomes learning how to be devoted and loyal to your corporate home without losing your independence and loyalty to yourself.

It's tough. "Marriage" is a natural and very real evolution from that very first day you say, "I do . . . want that job" because:

- You become a part of a group that knows each other very well.
- Your services become specialized within the company.
- You become used to the corporate culture and how your particular company does things.
- The pyramid narrows near the top, and the higher up you go, the fewer jobs and opportunities you'll find outside your corporate union.

The people, the benefits, the weekly paycheck, and the routine become as comfortable as an old shoe. "I" subtly shifts to "we." "*We're* proud of her," a branch manager enthused about a member of her staff. "She's been with *us* for six years and has grown as a real person." We not only reap the rewards of corporate union, but we like to show it off.

This is not necessarily a bad thing. "Marrying" your corporation can be the best thing in life. Just as a good marriage in your personal life encourages growth and satisfaction, so does a corporate marriage bound by love and faith. As one extremely successful human resources manager said, "I never thought I'd end up in personnel. When I was transferred out of line management into this department, I felt like the company had thrown me a curve. I was sure it wouldn't work out. But I believe that if you are going to make it in a company, you have to say 'whither thou goest.' And here I am—satisfied. I've prospered and the company has prospered."

Not everyone can have that much faith in his or her company. Many marriages are based on convenience or fear, with money or security being the most important factor. Ideally, as in all good relationships, you should be with your company because you *want* to, not because it's too frightening or complicated to leave.

The key to a good corporate union is dual loyalty: loyalty to yourself *and* to the corporation. You have to care about yourself first, because when push comes to shove, your company will put the bottom line before you. I interviewed personnel managers who fired dozens of loyal employees. I interviewed managers who fired their best friends. It's not shocking. It's business. And *your* first order of business is to take care of yourself.

It's vital for you to understand your relationship in the corporate family so that you can make your home a happy one, both for yourself and for the powers-that-be.

In the next few chapters you'll meet some other members of your corporate family and see where you fit in . . . and why.

Chapter 2

Boss-Parenting: Managers as Parents

"A successful manager makes it on the shoulders of his subordinates, not on the skeletons."

—Owner of executive search
firm in San Francisco

It begins the first day in a new job. You've deliberated over what to wear, perhaps laying it out the night before. You've tried to get a good, solid eight hours, but you've probably spent the night tossing and turning.

Let's face it. You're scared. The clock has turned back and you're the new kid in a new neighborhood. It's exciting, but it's unknown. There are new people to meet, new rules to learn, new routes to map out. And above all, there's the Boss. The one person who can make you—or break you.

In every family, there's a parent. And in every job, there's a boss. Like Mom and Dad, they set the rules and tell you what to do. If you don't obey, you'll be punished. If you're good, you're rewarded—with more "allowance" or, if you're *really* good, with the keys to the company car.

15

The boss dominates your early corporate life. You need "Mommy-boss" or "Daddy-boss" to help set down roots in your new home, to provide an anchor while you're memorizing the names in the directory or wandering down mazelike corridors full of self-sufficient strangers. Dependency flourishes while you're in this childlike state, and for many people it's a Parent Trap that can continue throughout a career.

External pressures also foster this Parent Trap: cutthroat competition for jobs and raises, a shaky economy, and a big mortgage or hospital bill that makes you need the job so much that you're terrified of losing it. Once again, the boss-parent looms up as a savior, the one person who can keep the cruel, callous world at bay.

Recruiters tell me they are most successful at luring employees away from indifferent managers, ones who are not particularly close or involved with their people. It's very hard *not* to get involved with your boss if you're on the receiving end. They represent power and protection.

Like parents, bosses can be mean or understanding, manipulative or demanding, authoritarian or indifferent, compassionate or even cruel. However, one characteristic all bosses share is the ability to get their hooks into their employees—and that means you.

A GOOD BOSS IS HARD TO FIND . . .

Good bosses are the oases in a world of Parent Traps. They:

- Get you raises and perks
- Help you grow with honest feedback and on-the-job training
- Nurture and protect you without being overly permissive
- Motivate more with praise than criticism

- Give you a second chance
- Demand and inspire loyalty

We all want good bosses, and they are out there. A commercial artist named Marcy was lucky enough to find one. Just when she thought she'd never get a job in the tough market artists face, she found a woman who gave her a break. Marcy plunged in, determined to show her new boss that she'd made the right decision. When her first major effort was rejected by the client, her boss called her into her office. Marcy braced herself for the chewing out she was sure would follow. But instead of condemnation, Marcy's boss simply said, "It was a tough assignment for a new person. I'll help you fix it up."

Now, *that* is a good boss. She has the potential to become a "Superboss," the mentor who guides your career, not just your job.

But Superbosses create their own kind of Parent Trap. With all that warm family feeling, you might never want to leave home —even for a better job. Good bosses can inspire more than loyalty. They can inspire guilt—and a fear of the outside world. Who is comfortable leaving a situation that's secure, where you find the welcome mat out whenever you need it? Who wouldn't feel disloyal taking a headhunter's call behind a good boss's back? And there's always the chance that that great job offer could turn out to be a snake pit, at least compared to the good deal you've got right now.

Marcy's relationship with her Superboss deepened over the years. With time, Marcy's expertise matched that of her boss. There was little left to learn in her current position, and she longed for new challenges. But she felt guilty even *thinking* about leaving. For over a year Marcy kept trying to work something out on the job, but her boss ignored all her suggestions. "I asked for new responsibilities. I asked if we could become partners. But she insisted on keeping control." Marcy finally left to start her own company. Five years after the fact she told me, "It was rough to break away. I knew it would hurt her. She had taught me so much, and now I was part of the competition. If I hadn't given birth to my daughter and needed more flexible hours than my boss was willing to give, I'd probably be there still. It was hell to leave."

Someday you may have to cut that umbilical cord. Maybe, like Marcy, you've learned all a good boss can teach you, and for your own growth you have to move on. Or maybe you've realized that even though you love your boss, the company or field just isn't for you.

And here's the crucial crunch. Real parents are supposed to prepare their children to leave home; corporate parents *don't*. They consciously work at inspiring that loyalty for their own good and the good of the company. Even the best boss will probably try to block your departure if you're needed for the work at hand.

A client I'll call Charlie had a great rapport with his boss. They worked hard together every day, and several nights a month they'd go out for a drink. His boss was always considerate. He got good raises for Charlie over the years, and he taught Charlie a lot. But politics got rough, and Charlie knew it was only a matter of time before his boss retired, leaving him easy prey for his boss's enemies. Despite all this, Charlie couldn't make up his mind to leave—even after he received a fantastic job offer. Finally, with much deliberation, Charlie said yes. He waltzed into his boss's office to tell him the good news, fully expecting his "buddy" to congratulate him warmly.

Instead of a champagne toast and a friendly slap on the back, his boss was frigid. He gave Charlie five minutes and coldly asked him to leave.

Poor Charlie. He didn't understand that his boss was simply acting like a corporate parent. Why should he be happy at the prospect of training somebody new for Charlie's spot? In fact, when Charlie's right-hand man left *him* a few years down the road, he finally understood his Superboss's reaction.

Occasionally good bosses will be glad for you, but usually only if you've already left their department or if you wouldn't have succeeded in the company anyway. More often than not, even the most rational of managers will feel deserted and betrayed.

Good-byes are always tinged with loss. You won't have to feel guilty about leaving a good boss as long as you remember that just as your boss's first responsibility is to his career, yours is to yourself. Parting *can* be a sweet sorrow.

... BUT A BAD BOSS IS HARD TO LEAVE

It's easy to understand why people want to stay with good boss-parents. What's hard to believe is how many people find it tough to leave the bad ones. Personnel experts are now beginning to discover what psychologists have always known: bad parents often inspire more blind loyalty than good ones.

The complex relationships between bad bosses and their subordinates are often an extension of ancient childhood struggles. The situations vary from individual to individual, but chances are that the unresolved issues you left behind in your real home will resurface in conflicts with your boss. Boss-parents will push the same buttons your real parents did. Unconsciously, you'll re-create your early childhood dramas. Here are some examples I've found in my practice:

1. If you felt abandoned or afraid a parent would leave when you were young . . . you might be afraid it will happen again. So you try to be very, very good and work very, very hard to please your bosses—no matter how belittling they are.

2. If a parent didn't help you resolve your teen-age rebellions . . . you just might shift that rebellion onto the workplace, self-

19

destructively lashing out at your boss or refusing to obey company rules.

3. If you have an unresolved need for a loving, caring parent . . . you might blindly idealize your bosses—even if they are mean or cruel.

4. If your parents were constantly criticizing your behavior . . . you might not only identify with critical bosses, but continually try to placate them and win their approval.

Psychologists label these examples of irrational loyalty toward demeaning, uncaring bosses "repetition compulsion." Bad bosses set an insidious Parent Trap by creating an unhappy instant replay of the bad old days. Just as children from alcoholic families often marry alcoholics in an attempt to resolve old wounds, so do children with unresolved family tensions seek out bad bosses time and again. They are determined to triumph this time and set the problem right.

Consider Denise, a computer expert with drive—and an overly critical mother who never gave praise. When I first met Denise, she was stuck in a job that was beneath her talents, with a demeaning boss to boot. One day, long after she'd left her real family, Denise talked to me about her boss: "Joan is just like my mother. If I can lick this one, if I can come out shining, then I can do a lot of other things. If I just don't let her get to me. If I can only get through to her . . ."

Denise couldn't win her mother's approval, so she re-created the situation at work, wasting valuable energy on an impossible ambition. It wasn't easy for her to give up the dream of winning over a woman who couldn't be won. But she did. Denise finally changed firms, with an increase in pay and a boss who acts more like a good mother than a bad one.

There's an addictive side to this psychological Parent Trap as well. Stressful situations—such as the challenge of pleasing a demeaning boss—produce adrenaline. We can actually become addicted to that adrenaline rush—and to the bad boss who gives it to us. Like the gambler at the roulette table, we want to feel the high that comes from the game. Normal life—and normal relationships—seem dull by comparison.

How can you tell if you're replaying your childhood in an unhealthy relationship with your boss? Be suspicious if:

- You talk about your boss all the time, or think about him or her obsessively.
- You're in a managerial position but find yourself doing subservient duties inappropriate to your status. (Women are especially susceptible to this because "being a good girl" is much more ingrained than "being a good boy.")
- You find yourself constantly trying to get praise and approval.
- You feel blocked or frustrated by your boss, but you're not writing that résumé or implementing any kind of effective job search.
- You look forward to the adrenaline rush associated with an upcoming confrontation between you and your boss.

If you find yourself reacting irrationally to your boss-parent, the best thing to do is think back to your own childhood and try to diagnose the situation. Are you idolizing your boss because he represents the good father you never had? Are you still trying to win approval from an overbearing mother? A helpful hint to clear the confusing air of the Parent Trap for proper analysis is to stop calling your boss "boss." Try saying "department head" or "supervisor." It puts the two of you in a more professional relationship and helps you see the boss as less of an imposing, omnipotent authority figure.

MASTERMINDS

Like Gertrude Stein's rose, "a good department head is a good department head" ad infinitum. But a bad boss comes in three

21

basic shapes: manipulative, authoritarian, or cruel—and each one has its own particular Parent Trap that can ensnare you and keep you coming back for more:

THE MIGHTY OZ

These bosses are the mighty manipulators, and they rarely are what they seem. When you first walk into their offices, they hold out their hands for a warm handshake. A smile is always on their faces. They are so sympathetic, considerate, and enthusiastic that they seem like Superbosses. But give them time. Eventually their real personalities come through. They'll take all the credit for themselves—when you did all the work. When the going gets tough, these manipulators get going—and leave you holding the bag. And when it's time for you to leave, the Mighty Oz bosses will make you feel guilty. They'll be shocked by your affrontery or cry great crocodile tears until you promise to stay.

Their tricks work more often than not. As Pat Heanue, owner of Vantage Careers, a recruiting firm in White Plains, New York, told me: "People come to me because they are dissatisfied. I find them a good job, but when they go to quit, the boss says he *needs* them. It creates guilt. He tells them it's tax season or it's marketing week, or no one new could possibly understand the job. It's ridiculous, but it works. I've seen hundreds of people turn down good job offers because of it."

John, an efficient and cheerfully rumpled office manager, was a victim of a Mighty Oz not too long ago. He never complained about his low salary and infrequent raises because he believed his boss really cared about him and would pay him more if he only could. After all, his boss always took the time to have friendly chats. He took John to lunch. He even gave him tickets to football games. But one day John accidentally noticed a junior employee's paycheck, which was more than his. John was stunned. He felt utterly betrayed by the "good" boss who'd taken advantage of his undemanding nature. And he even learned later that his boss had given him the football tickets when no one else had wanted them.

As managerial psychologist Harold Leavitt points out, a manipulative boss "exploits peoples' needs for approval, support, recognition, dependency, and participation. [He] plays us for suckers." A Mighty Oz makes a career out of looking like a good guy. Most people never realize Oz is a "humbug" until the hooks are in and it's too late.

THE GENERALISSIMO

Generalissimos seem like heroic leaders, but they're really rigid, rank-pulling bullies. While good bosses seek a unified front, the Generalissimos want nothing less than a dictatorship. Power is their passion and they love to tell you what to do and how to do it. The authoritarians of an organization, they rule with an iron hand.

The Generalissimos keep people running to their beck and call because they offer structure and security that both debilitates *and* binds at the same time. In a world where everyone seems confused, there's a certain comfort in working for Generalissimos even if they are arrogant and never give your creative ideas a fair hearing. Sometimes it looks as if they are the only ones who know what they're talking about and know what's right. They provide so *much* direction that you never have to ask a question or take a chance. But there is a price to pay for this steel-walled security: you stop thinking for yourself and you're no longer free to make you *own* decisions.

George is a case in point. A thirty-two-year-old adult, he still felt like a weak, controlled child when it came to his authoritarian boss-parent—who also happened to be his father. "He'd insult my brother and me in public if we didn't do things just his way."

This Generalissimo paid his sons next to nothing, but on occasion he'd come through with a brand-new car or equally generous present to keep them grateful. He kept all the power for himself, never delegating any real responsibility and never letting

23

his sons see the books of the family-owned manufacturing plant. When rebellion threatened, he dangled, "All this will be yours someday."

For a long time George didn't realize he was treated badly. "It was really hard to extricate myself. It took me five years to leave, and I might not have unless my wife pushed me. My brother's been saying he's going to leave for two years, but he's afraid to tell our father."

If you think you're working for a Generalissimo, make sure that he or she really is authoritarian and not merely authoritative. Think "always." Are your projects and suggestions *always* getting squashed? Do you *always* have to do things the Generalissimo's way? Are you *always* left in the dark?

But the last, and by no means least, bad boss to consider is never too hard to recognize in any light:

MOMMIE DEAREST

Authoritarian Generalissimo bosses will only criticize when they want to save face or preserve their power, but Mommie Dearests will find something wrong whenever they can. Nasty to the core, these people use sarcasm or abuse when a plain yes or no will do. It doesn't matter whether you worked all night, slaving over some project, or whether you relentlessly searched out the fact that saved the day, you'll never even get a small "thank you" from your Mommie Dearest boss. He or she will surely find some mistake and point it out to you—in excruciating detail.

You can feel your confidence wither when a Mommie Dearest sinks in her claws. But how do you know it's your boss and not you? A Fortune 100 personnel director gave me a good distinction: "Are they extremely demanding or unfair? If they're just demanding, that's okay. It's a good way to learn. But if they're unfair, demeaning, and belittling on a personal level, that's another thing."

A true Mommie Dearest can hurt—badly. So why put up with

this abuse? For two simple reasons: 1) many people feel they need to be pushed and criticized into performing well; and 2) a boss-parent who is really good at criticism destroys the self-esteem you need to find another job. Mommie Dearests create so many self-doubts that employees who work under them begin to believe they can't do anything right. They are the fertilizer that makes those "repetition compulsions" flourish. As one M.B.A. said worriedly, "This person knows me well, and if he doesn't appreciate me, maybe no one else will."

My friend Peter was lucky. He was able to get out of his Mommie Dearest's hold and go on to become the youngest executive on his new company's board of directors. But he still talks about his first boss: "My boss would walk into my office, close the door, and start insulting me. It took a long time to realize that the reason I felt so bad was because he'd personalized his criticism. He'd say 'You're stupid' or 'You're selfish' to me all the time."

When Peter tells this story, he changes from the successful businessman he is today and becomes once again that hurting "child." It's been seventeen years, and he's still bearing the painful mental scars of his Mommie Dearest boss.

PEOPLE VERSUS PROFIT

With so much going for good bosses and so little for bad ones, why do companies keep the villains around at all? Because as long as things are running smoothly and profits are high, they:

a. Don't know about the bad boss
b. Don't care
c. Keep the bad boss around because he or she is getting good results
d. All of the above

If you've answered "All of the above," you're probably right. Mommie Dearest or Mighty Oz bosses, for example, can be extremely polite and charming to superiors. The higher-ups *never* see their nasty side, only their unlucky subordinates do. Generalissimos, on the other hand, walk around like prima donnas, but their demanding qualities often bring in fast results and short-term profit. A board of directors would never be so foolish as to fire them. In fact, they are often *afraid* to let a Generalissimo go. An extremely experienced Fortune 500 executive put it this way: "There is a concern in corporations that building business and building people are antithetical. They worry that if they fire all the tough people, they'll end up with a weak organization."

People-oriented or profit-oriented. It's a controversy still being pulled apart on the corporate battlefields. Can a boss get ahead being both nurturing *and* concerned for the bottom line?

"Years ago we cleaned house and made it clear that promotion and pay depends on how well you build people," a personnel director at a huge electronics firm told me. "At the same time, a guy came in who was very macho, very arrogant, and overly demanding. If anybody complained, he thought they were weak, and he'd discard them. When he became a vice-president, his problems with people finally became clear to management. It took a long time to get rid of him even though more than half the managers under him dropped out. He was clever and smart, but he was ruining good people."

YOU KNOW BEST

The people-versus-profit picture will be hashed and rehashed in the boardroom. In the smaller realm, there's still you and your boss. You do have responsibilities as part of the organization. The corporation is paying you a salary. In return, you are expected to try to please your boss-parent. Your boss-parent rightfully expects your loyalty, especially if he or she helped to refine your corporate skills.

But your first loyalty must be to yourself. When healthy people are faced with a terrible boss, they'll say, "Who needs this?" They might leave, or they just might stay on and learn everything they can without getting emotionally involved in the Parent Trap struggle. They'll reap the benefits of the job before cutting the cord.

Understanding the relationship you have with your boss is vital to corporate success, and it helps immensely when the tables are turned and *you* become a boss-parent yourself. . . .

MODERN MATURITY

Climb the corporate ladder and you'll soon become a boss-parent yourself. Unless you were born a Bad Seed, or you get your kicks with black leather and whips, you're not going to go out of your way to be a bad boss. But to become a good boss-parent instead of a Mommie Dearest, you have to keep in mind those days when you were "growing up."

"When you grow in a corporation," said a successful executive I interviewed, "you have to have a really good memory. You have to *want* to remember what you were like as a staff assistant. How you wanted a piece of the pie. How eager you were for the raises, responsibility, and perks like expensive business lunches or the sales conferences in Hawaii. You have to remember to share these things with *your* assistants now."

In your early years as boss-parent, this kind of thinking comes naturally. After all, it wasn't so long ago that you were there. If you're close in age, the feeling is more one of older brother or sister than parent-child. The higher you rise, the more conscious determination you must bring to your parenting role:

"Now that I've got a hundred people under me, some I hardly know, it stretches credulity to care about each one of them personally," a generous and caring boss-father told me. "I can't possibly know all about their personal lives and how they bring it to the office. But I try. It brings in good results."

This executive has few problems balancing people with the bottom line. For others, this can turn into the "Catch-22" that makes for their undoing, a Parent Trap in reverse.

Consider the case of Ellen, an executive from Atlanta who finds boss-parenting at the top tough: "I've risen up the corporate ladder so high that I can't talk to people as if they are my team anymore. We are too big. I can't even talk about what is best for clients. All I can think about is the bottom line."

For people like Ellen, becoming a boss-parent can be a rude awakening. For others it's a role they never want—or will— assume.

Though most people in the corporate world aspire to become boss-parents themselves, there are exceptions—often writers, artists, supersalesmen, scientists, and technicians—for whom managing people seems more a burden than a sign of success. They have no desire to lead or control others. They just want to be free to do good work. In highly structured corporations, they'll never command the "big bucks," and sometimes they're forced out. But many companies today are creating "dual ladders" for these nonparents, where they can work on their technical or creative endeavors while still finding corporate success.

Whatever your corporation's advancement policies, there will always be a day of reckoning: either getting a new boss-parent, becoming one yourself, or going the nonparent route. Like any rite of passage, each presents stumbling blocks that can trip you up if you're not prepared. It's crucial, both personally and professionally, to understand your boss-parent relationships to achieve success in the corporate world. Armed with that knowledge, you too can have—and be—a Superboss.

Now let's turn from your department head and go to the other members of your corporate family tree. . . .

Chapter 3

Sibling Rivalry and Support: Your Colleagues at Work

"I was very friendly with many of the people I worked with. But after I left, I never saw them again."
—Former sales manager,
Worldwide cosmetics firm

"We are like brothers and sisters here. We share ideas and we help each other out. When the boss goes on a rampage, we prop each other up."

"I can't wait to get to the office each day. I like the work and I really like the people. It's the place where I'm appreciated . . . where I get praise."

The boss-parent might be at the center of your universe when you're first starting out, but the friends you make on the job are the ones you talk to when things go wrong or right. Though your boss is your superior, your friends are on an equal plane. They are the "brothers" and "sisters" with whom you spend most of your time.

And a good relationship with your peers at work is one of the best benefits a job can offer, especially in our fast-moving world

29

where friendships are so hard to make and sustain. Your corporate siblings are the "kindred spirits" who share the same anxieties. They share the same pleasures and pains from company policy. They can feel your triumphs because they have felt them too. They can cut through needless explanations when you show them the unfriendly memo you've just received, knowing who it is from and why it was written in a particular tone. They instantly understand what that new project assignment means. They are living, breathing, and participating in the same corporate family as yourself.

Twenty years ago a study was conducted at AT&T among their managers to discover what they considered the most important component of their working lives. In a world where the Organization Man looked up to his superiors, it's not surprising that the researchers found "deference to authority" their main focus. But that same study was recently done again at AT&T. This time around, "deference to authority" dropped 50 percent while "loyalty to workplace peers" took the number one slot—telltale proof that the relationships we have with our corporate "siblings" are becoming more and more important to the health and happiness of our corporate homes.

THE GOLDEN CONNECTION

"We all work hard, and there's no backstabbing in our group," says a purchasing agent at a medium-size firm. "Afterward we go out for a couple of drinks and some talk. A lot of wives and husbands are waiting at home, but it doesn't matter. It feels great!"

Like no other feeling in the world. But there's something very transient about these corporate friendships as well. Your conversations, your goals, and your very lives all revolve around the corporation. People who retain friendships after leaving home are more the exception than the rule because:

Sibling Rivalry and Support: Your Colleagues at Work

1. There are no real blood ties.
Past associations with a corporation get very stale very quickly if you're not there. Once I went back to visit my "brothers and sisters" at an old job only to discover they had quickly adopted the new person who sat at my desk. An extra chair had to be squeezed in for me at "our regular table" at the restaurant around the corner. It was painfully obvious that physically and emotionally there was no place there for me anymore.

2. Corporate life is dynamic and fast-changing.
The players and the situations move around so quickly that by the time you pay a return visit, the office stage is different. A man in corporate culture shock told me, "Only six months after I left my job, I went to a party and ran into a lot of people I used to work with. It was terrific at first, but then I realized we had very little in common anymore. I had never even heard of half the people they were talking about."

3. Corporate pressures are extremely intense.
And it's hard for any outsider—and that includes you when you leave—to really understand what's going on.

4. Corporate success demands much time and energy.
It's very difficult to sustain the same intimacy and closeness without regular contact at the office.

5. You become part of "the outside"—rejecter or rejected.
If you were fired, you become an instant pariah. People are afraid your bad luck will rub off on them. If you leave of your own free will, you've abandoned the group. And worse, if you move on to a rival corporation, you are a traitor. There are many corporate secrets and strategies that can't be discussed around you.

6. With corporate friends, there's always a façade to maintain.
Even your closest corporate "brothers and sisters" are still rivals

31

for promotion and power. There's always the nagging thought that what they know can be used against you if you show too much of the "real" face—the one that includes weaknesses and doubts—that you can reveal to tried and true friends. You share experiences, not your souls. This basic distinction makes for friendships that do not endure with time.

Why question your corporate friendships? Because relationships at work *can* stop you from looking out for your own best interest. As one financial analyst put it: "Your friendships are very, very deep with these people. But it's because the time is right and the place is right. There's a sense that if I leave, I'll lose this." You don't want to lose the friendships, so you don't leave the family.

FACTS OF LIFE

When you call up a real friend to announce your promotion, that friend will be happy for you and start planning a celebration dinner. But your corporate siblings won't always cheer your success if it means you move over them—or out. Instead, they are more likely to feel threatened or betrayed. The peer pressure office friends exert, whether unconscious or overt, can halt caring people in their tracks, because leaving means less contact with that friendly social group and professional support network, and because leaving declares you want something different from your peers.

An editor I know at a large-circulation women's magazine is a case in point. She was elated when she snagged a job interview at a rival magazine for a senior position. She made the mistake of sharing her excitement with a staff member who had been with the firm for over thirty years. "She was shocked by the news. She told me I had so much to lose if I left. I was shaken—and I began to wonder if maybe she was right." Fortunately, my editor friend realized in time that the older staffer was only voicing her own fears: that she felt lucky to have a job and was terrified to leave that security behind. "If I left, it would undermine everything she stood for."

As you rise up in the corporate ranks, building a nuclear family of your own as a department head parent, your social life may become less involved with the company. Even if social ties fade, other bonds can replace them. The higher up you move, the harder it is to leave that invaluable network of siblings who'll put in a good word for you with the president or get that requisition order out fast. As one senior executive told me: "It took me years to build up my people connections here. There's no way I could come in at my level and replace all that." He's been less and less happy at work lately, but he's turned down several good offers. Leaving the security of his peer group network would be as wrenching as a divorce, and he can't cut loose.

From networks to drinks after work, sibling support provides security in your corporate home. But there's another element to your corporate friendships that's just as strong a "hook." Support makes life comfortable, but rivalry makes life exciting.

THE SPICE OF LIFE

As in any family, corporate "brothers and sisters" vie for Mommy and Daddy's attention—in the form of money and the next rung up the ladder. You might be friends with your corporate siblings, but you're still rivals at heart.

Competition and camaraderie can be an intoxicating combination. As an associate in a large law firm said: "The concept of family is true here. I'm in a small group within a large partnership, and we really are a family. We all work long hours. We all work very intensely with each other. But it's also a high-stakes rivalry. People are helping you out—while they're in competition with you."

The mix is addictive. Support and rivalry, like the other kinds of stress I've talked about, keep the adrenaline flowing. It makes for a highly charged atmosphere that can hook you into staying even when you shouldn't. A division head in an engineering firm told me, "It's great working with eagles instead of turkeys. Everyone's so smart." With that kind of thinking, everything else seems like a step down.

From their earliest days, corporations have encouraged rivalry to make people work harder. People want to win, and the company provides the incentive.

Automobile companies were among the first to understand the power of internal competition. They broke their giant organizations down into competing divisions. At General Motors, Chevrolet competes as strongly with Pontiac as it does with Ford. Consumer goods corporations have used similar competitive tactics with their brand management systems. Colgate-Palmolive, for example, makes several different detergents—all with similar ingredients. The main differences between one detergent and another are their packaging and promotion.

Sometimes rivalry is seen as a game of status, complete with a dangling prize. I remember what a young buyer for the Federated Department Stores chain told me about her family's sibling rivalry. "The general merchandise manager doles out the money to the different departments. The more money you get, the more you can buy. When a hot item like a new Calvin Klein jean comes out, we *all* want it, from sportswear to the designer shops on another floor. There's a lot of backbiting. Lots of competition. But no one cares about the nasty stuff if you produce." Whichever buyer comes out on top in sales receives not only a promotion, but the right to wear the symbol of success: a black mink coat.

Nor is the business world the exclusive battleground for sibling rivalry. Nonprofit organizations are not above competition.

Here's an example from academia. A professor I know was worried about his future in the college where he taught. "Everyone competes for tenure. We all want it desperately, not only for security, but because it means you're 'in the club.' A friend of mine was just granted tenure, and the very next day she received her first invitation for drinks with the faculty dean and the president of the college. The powers-that-be even create a system that makes nontenured professors feel like children. They call us 'junior' faculty even though many of us are older than the members of the tenured 'senior' faculty. They hold out tenure as a great prize, and we are all so obsessed with it that we devote our whole lives to getting it. The rivalry is so strong that we never question why it's important—or why our salaries are so low."

Competition is as much a part of American tradition as apple juice. But the race to win can sometimes do more harm than good. "Junior" professors might stay obsessed and underpaid, and corporate siblings might stay in a home gone bad just to see the game played out.

Alice was one of these players. A young sales rep with no seniority in a failing manufacturing firm, she refused even to think about looking for another job when budget-cut rumors were confirmed. Luckily, she survived the first round. Instead of using the extra breathing space to start her search, Alice stayed put. She couldn't quit until the purge was finished. She had to find out whether or not she'd be a winner—allowed to stay on in a company that was heading for a fall. As Alice admitted to me, "I had to find out if I'd be one of the favorites or not."

Rivalry also exists at the top. It's how many companies today are choosing presidents. Chief executive officers often pick several contenders and let them do battle to see who comes out on top. Besides creating unproductive politics, this kind of rivalry race makes for short-term profit-thinking. Sound long-term growth can take second place to the Big Splash. "Is this the way to train successors?" asks Thorne Foster, president of a San Francisco search firm. "Is this really a way to do business? Performance and a proven track record over the years should be the criteria instead."

Clean competition can be as deeply satisfying as your corporate friendships. If you have a good support system *plus* a good shot at winning the prize in the rivalry game, you won't want to think about leaving home. But you have to be aware of the "rivalry hooks." Group pressure or obsessive thoughts or even an adrenaline high can keep you in a race you no longer want to win—or no longer have a chance of winning.

THE GOOD, THE BAD, AND THE FAMILY

Like your real brothers and sisters, your corporate siblings have both good and bad within them. Support and rivalry. Generosity and greediness. Courage and cowardice. Your colleagues, not unlike your relatives, come with the territory. Your coworkers become an integral part of your life.

As attached as we grow to our corporate family, there still comes a time when we might have to leave. Making that decision is made even harder because friendship is so intense. It means a real loss: giving up so much of what we know and who we know. This bittersweet texture is best summed up by a man who left his corporation for a better job: "I roamed the halls, knowing I was leaving my friends behind. I knew I'd never see most of them again. And I knew I was leaving a part of my life forever." To live up to your potential and grow within the business world, sometimes you have to leave home.

It's natural to get close to your corporate siblings, especially those with whom you work side by side. This intensity is the fuel that fires team spirit, the "us against them" motivation that whips us into action and keeps us fiercely tied together. Because, for better or worse, team spirit is such a powerful magnet, and because consultants are teaching corporations how to foster team spirit to decrease turnover and increase productivity, it's a topic that deserves its own chapter. . . .

Chapter 4

Team Spirit and
the New Maternalism

"Smart companies make employees think they're working
on a team. It keeps pay low, unions out, and productivity
high."
                              —Research chemist,
                              Pharmaceutical company

Management consultant Dan Adams points out: "Team
building has been around forever. Christ did it." American
corporations have long understood the rewards of competition,
but only recently have they learned the implications of this age-
old system of support.

"There's a new movement afoot," says a senior manager in a
Fortune 100 corporation. "Team approach. It's what companies
are using to give people more incentive, to really get in and make
a contribution. They're also making managers feel like owners,
through stock plans or buyouts. The new concept is, 'You're part
of a team and you're becoming an owner of the company.' "

Good managers instinctively breed loyalty in their subordinates. As personnel agency owner Pat Heanue explains, "The
best ones have always been natural, strong leaders who make
their people feel part of a team." Today team building has moved
beyond instinct to become conscious corporate strategy. Consul-

tants are now teaching these skills to corporations who, in turn, are applying them to raise productivity and to keep employees content.

A case in point is the strategy consultant Dan Adams used in the media department of an advertising agency. This particular department was considered a short-term stepping-stone to more lucrative positions elsewhere. Many people who worked there couldn't wait to leave. They hated the work. They held up their supervisors for raises. Adams first hired people who liked media and who liked their job at the agency. He then organized them into small teams. He gave them more responsibility than they had before to do their jobs better and a significant voice in the goal-setting process. Turnover dropped drastically. Managers were no longer hit with unreasonable demands for raises. Better people were staying in the media department.

Team building clearly works, and team spirit is the ultimate in family feeling, corporate style. But how did something that just came naturally to good managers evolve into a trainable skill and high corporate art? For the answers to these questions, let's go back a bit. "In the beginning . . ."

A HISTORY LESSON

Once upon a time, in the Land of Opportunity, we were all corporate children under the mercy of the stern, stingy, father-figure Paternalist, who founded and ran the company. These Paternalists were proud of the fact that they could call every single worker by name. They paid low wages, benefits were paltry, but they bestowed smiles and small gifts onto their employees, even throwing in a turkey at Christmas. In return for their beneficence, these owners expected gratitude and submission. For lifelong devotion, we received lifelong jobs. Father took care of all of us as long as we knew our places.

As these corporations flourished and grew, so did the

founders. After they died, eventually family ownership usually gave way to professional management. Paternalism was no longer a one-man rule. It was spruced up and integrated into sophisticated company policy. The 1950s Organization Man became the new symbol of the successful corporate executive, the man who still pledged his working life to the company but who was rewarded, not with Christmas turkeys and pats on the head, but with money, promotions, and a sense of pride.

Yet it came to pass in the free-thinking '60s that gray flannel suits and other accouterments of corporate success were no longer ideals to strive for. The "me generation" was born, and Paternalism became a dirty word. No one wanted to marry the corporation anymore.

But Paternalism refused to die. When the inflation and recession that signaled the 1970s hit in full force, corporate salaries and benefits became even more generous—and too attractive to ignore. Paternalism changed and grew as corporate America turned to the successful Japanese companies for inspiration.

THE SUSHI CONNECTION

As William Ouchi taught us in Theory Z, "the Japanese understand how to organize and manage people at work. It's not necessarily *harder* work that's needed, but a different social organization. The Japanese built up their quality circles—work groups where a person's ideas benefit both the individual and the group, where there's an intimacy, a caring, support, and a disciplined unselfishness." The ultimate team.

Thanks to this team effort, corporations in the Land of the Rising Sun have consistently had high productivity, practically nonexistent turnover, and morale that doesn't drop.

Part of their tremendous success is built into the Japanese culture. They are not above blacklisting and other methods of persuasion to keep people in their corporate homes. Obviously, these tactics are alien to the American way. We've only latched on to the positive Japanese elements: the loyalty, discipline, and adherence to authority as exemplified by the samurai. But before you get the idea that the samurai warrior inspired the New Paternalism, listen to what management expert Peter Drucker discovered:

"Again and again I've been laughed at in Japan when I talk about Japanese management embodying Japanese values. 'Don't you realize,' my Japanese friends say, 'that we are simply adapting what IBM has done all along? When we started to rebuild Japan in the 1950s, we looked around for the most successful company we could find. It is IBM, isn't it?' " Team-building precepts were originally stamped "Made in America," but it took the Japanese to borrow them and turn them into high art.

THE MODERN FAMILY

Thanks to the Japanese, we've brought home an improved version of our own traditions of team spirit and loyalty. We've added a little here, subtracted a little there. It's the new American management, but no one quite knows what to call it. Experts still talk about paternalism, but listening to managers mention "Mother IBM" and "Mother Procter" and Time Inc. as "the great Mother tit," it seems clear that the gender of corporate America is changing. The new paternalism is really maternal.

Instead of the stingy, turkey-giving "Dickens Inc." of long ago or the mindless conformity of the 1950s, we have a nurturing mother who asks, "Are you happy? Are you growing? Do you have enough benefits?" Mother is no fool. She knows that happy families stay together.

This New Maternalism is not turning corporate America into single-parent matriarchies. Far from it. Mother has her counterbalance in the hard-nosed leaders who rise to the top. No longer old-school gentlemen, these new heroes exemplify the tough, skillful, All-American coach who leads his team to victory.

Welcome to the new corporate family, where, for the first time in our history, corporate homes have a complete family unit with a mother, a father, and a whole host of sibling team members. The modern age has arrived in full force.

THE PSYCHOLOGICAL BASE

Although this new, team-oriented maternalism has only evolved into corporate policy within the past twenty years, industrial psychologists and researchers have been on the case much longer. In the 1920s the famous Hawthorne studies proved that productivity increases when workers know management cares about them and notices what they're doing.

In the 1960s psychologist Frederick Herzberg took the Hawthorne studies one step further. He discovered that real motivation comes from real responsibility, not simply good salaries and good fringe benefits. Even with the best raises and corporate perks, most workers would not perform well unless they were given room to excel.

These and other research studies became the basis for the "management by objective" policies now found in corporations, policies that state very clear goals and provide solid feedback on each employee's contribution to the "organizational mission." The best way to implement these policies is through the team approach, an effective, seductive, and quick way to give the maximum responsibility and visibility workers need to excel.

On a deeper level, the team approach also satisfies the "existential dualism" that spurs man on: the need to be part of something and the need to stand out. People have the dual need to be both a conforming member of a winning team *and* a star in their own right. The best teams select people who have certain skills and love using them. They're allowed to run wild with their expertise

42

while bound together in a common purpose, making a significant contribution to their own careers *and* the group as a whole. Thus the two contradictory drives—the existential dualism—are combined, creating one extremely powerful force.

THE A-TEAM

A salesman recently described his experience with his manufacturing firm's hell-bent attempts at instilling team spirit: "I went to a sales meeting, and the manager went crazy on this team theme. They brought in office people and technical people. They passed out football shirts with the name of the company printed across the front. The president was there, and he was introduced as the head coach. It was fun, it was exciting, and I liked meeting everyone. But there was no follow-through after that. It didn't change a thing."

Employees can see beyond the T-shirts and the logos on balloons. And after the hoopla dies down, there's more dissatisfaction than ever—and a real sense of disillusionment to boot. People *want* to belong, and team spirit taps into their need at a very deep level. They'll meet their company more than halfway, but ultimately the effort has to be sincere. To generate a real team spirit, much more is required than superficial meetings and a caring medical plan. The new team spirit found in good corporations today has taken

- the New Maternalism
- a strong leader
- team-building
- ownership identification

and turned these four interlocking pieces into a whole much greater than its parts.

THE NEW MATERNALISM, OR
MOTHER KNOWS BEST

There's no one like Mom. She cares about your health and happiness. She encourages you and wants you to grow. In New Maternalistic companies, employers believe that caring and nurturing go hand in hand with productivity. They'll give you the best benefit packages and vacation plans. They'll give you generous salaries; at the very least they'll be competitive with the leaders in the field. Owners today go beyond wanting to know your name. They want to know what you're thinking and what you're doing. They not only ask about your personal life, but offer to help.

And there is a method to this madness. If employees are going through personal crises, it can affect their work. "I identify my key people that I don't want to lose," a division manager in a consumer products firm explained. "I make sure they are financially well taken care of. I don't want them to worry about paying bills and wonder when or if they're going to get a raise. They'd waste a lot of time and energy if they worried about raises. I'd rather they spent the time more productively."

Another manager in a Fortune 500 company told me that his company "cares for people who get in trouble. We're proud of how far we go to take care of people who get into health, booze, or financial problems. We have very generous group health plans, and we go even further for a good person who's been loyal and one of the team. We have a slush fund to keep them on full salary forever if necessary."

Mother can also be very demanding and jealous of your time. She wouldn't mind if you stayed with her around the clock. As one Time Inc. employee said, "While you suckle, you get all the benefits, but you're expected to work extraordinary hours. You're judged by how long you work."

And work you will when a corporation offers so much and appreciates what you do. In fact, after your ten-hour day, many maternalistic companies provide lots of after-work activities to keep you going. There are tennis clinics for employees and their families. Softball teams. They'll send the whole brood to conferences together—anything to generate a family spirit and keep employees linked to their corporate home.

It's no wonder a New Maternalistic corporation makes you feel you'd be a fool to leave all that Mother can bestow.

A STRONG LEADER, OR
VINCE LOMBARDI IN A PINSTRIPE SUIT

The environment might be maternal, but the men and women who run the day-to-day operation and supply its spirit are tough: strong, purposeful, and dynamic. A strong leader creates a team's culture and values. He or she gives a reason for working those long, devoted hours beyond the weekly paycheck. A manager I interviewed put it this way: "Good leaders offer a vision of how people can be. They make their people excited about what they propose to do. They combine charisma, energy, and the self-possession to say, 'I know how the company should go. I know what people should do.' They make people really committed to the task at hand. A good leader encourages employees to take risks and be creative for the good of the organization."

Lee Iacocca became a leadership legend by taking over failing Chrysler and convincing workers to take a pay cut with a "charging up" philosophy that made everyone feel responsible for turning the company around. He generated so much enthusiasm and hope that Chrysler is now a strong competitor in the marketplace.

Strong leaders don't always have to have lofty goals to make a team work. Mary Kay, with her highly successful cosmetics line, appeals to people's love of money. Her goal is to make each one of her saleswomen rich. At one of her Dallas Convention Center seminars, it's not unusual to see the supersaleswomen of the year swathed in mink and diamonds. Millions of dollars are spent for lavish extravaganzas where Mary Kay saleswomen are inspired to get out there and make money.

45

Unfortunately, leaders don't walk around wearing white hats or black ones. Even experts have a hard time distinguishing a good leader from a bad one. A business professor told me about an eminent colleague's speech naming the best corporate leaders around today. Many of these same leaders appeared a few months later in a widely read business magazine's article about the worst managers in America.

Greatness is open to interpretation, but good leaders will always inspire loyalty and pull out their people's best.

TEAM BUILDING, OR
ONE FOR ALL AND ALL FOR ONE

An engineer I interviewed described his early years working for a large impersonal corporation: "I felt like an insignificant cog in a massive system. If I was sick for a month, my slot would be filled in and no one would ever know." This same engineer moved to a company that uses the team approach and he's a lot happier. "The team is wonderful because it brings a big corporation down to a very personal level. Everybody is known and everybody is noticed. Everybody is responsible for what they do and then they're left alone to do it."

In the best teams, each member feels vital, working for both corporate and individual gain. And when running smoothly, with cooperative and compatible talent, team building can have fantastic results.

Consider the team approach used to generate new business at Dancer Fitzgerald Sample, a large advertising agency. In the past, temporary teams were set up to pitch each new account. The chemistry and success quotient was hit or miss. Recently, the president of Dancer's New York office, Gary Susnjara, took over and made some changes that typify good team building.

He established a permanent group of people who excel at providing backup services and designing presentations. Then for each prospective account, he selects a team of account, creative, media, research, and promotion professionals who will actually run the business if they can win it. This is a high-visibility assignment. Each professional is given full responsibility for generating a piece of the presentation and every possible assistance from the permanent group. Susnjara allows each individual freedom to be creative, but the genuine enthusiasm he radiates fuses a cohesive team. Regardless of whether the account is large or small, if he decides DFS should pitch the account, he makes it clear that he *really* wants it. He is willing to work all night and all weekend along with his team, if necessary, and he is willing to commit the financial and personnel resources needed to do an excellent job. He says, "For every new business pitch, we create a 'super team' consisting of the permanent new business guys and the guys who will do the work. The key to our success is in the synergy created between the two groups."

As one of those "guys" (a generic term; the teams are coed) told me, "There is a lot of excitement and challenge with a new business presentation. Each one is a tough competitive match against several other good agencies. We work very hard to come up with the best strategic thinking, the best consumer motivation research, and the best marketing plan. Each pitch is a gamble, but with our team approach, it's poker instead of roulette." Actually, it sounds like stacking the deck: in a recent eighteen-month period, DFS pitched fourteen new accounts and won twelve of them!

OWNERSHIP IDENTIFICATION, OR A PIECE OF THE ROCK

Every company wants its people to feel a bond—and what better way than with strong identification. By the time you say "my company" instead of "the company," you're usually hooked and taking a proprietary interest in the company's success.

One of the best ways to get people to think "my" is with financial incentives. Stock options, a percent interest in the profits, and bonuses based both on personal performance and the performance of the corporation as a whole are all ways to build

47

up ownership identification. Financial packages can often just be a dangling carrot, offering vestiture only when one has been with the company for a period of time.

Ownership works best when financial incentives are combined with a personal involvement in decision making. An executive I know left a huge organization to join a smaller company where ownership, both financial and psychological, was a part of the "family" routine. The new place had a September to September bonus plan. Though the executive had only been aboard twelve days when the checks were issued, he still received $1000. "Not only are they generous with their money, but they give me a chance to be heard. In my old place, I could never bop in and talk to the chairman of the board. But they have an "open-door" policy here. I can see the Chairman whenever I want. He even asks my opinion. I feel like this is *my* place." He's not the only one. During a recent business downswing, no one jumped ship. Everyone pitched in and helped.

When all four pieces of the new team-spirit structure are working together at full throttle, it doesn't matter how many employees are listed in personnel. Large or small, executive recruiters find it almost impossible to lure people away from these places with any kind of inducement. Such devotion can be observed at huge corporations like IBM, with its extracurricular activities and open-door policies, and Hewlett-Packard, a firm that provides an environment people will happily trade for income. "Hewlett-Packard treats people well," says Jack Yelverton, president of a San Francisco executive search firm. "They hire smart people with good technical and people skills. And they let them use those skills to be successful. They maintain a high level of business ethics. It's highly prestigious to work there. It's like being in the Marines—people there have pride."

When I asked other executive recruiters about the companies where people stay put, they told me more of the same: the best ones don't necessarily pay the highest salaries, but they offer a combination of material and psychological benefits that just can't be beat.

For example, John Foster, a senior vice-president at the huge search firm Boyden Associates, talked about the team spirit found at Esprit, a small, fast-growing West Coast apparel company. He says, "Esprit instills loyalty by providing a creative environment and a whole host of cultural perks—free tickets for the theater, ballet, the newest art showings. They even encourage time off to get batteries recharged. And the company sponsors seminars where employees go off together to learn cooperation and interdependence."

Several experts mentioned how Eli Lily's excellent compensation packages and company spirit keep people steadfast and loyal. They're encouraged to speak their minds and walk into their boss's office at any time. "With companies like these," says Foster, "it's no wonder people refuse to leave."

A TRAITOR IN OUR MIDST

It feels great to be part of a healthy, cooperative team, in a good corporate family where all your psychological and material needs are met—*if* that's what you want. The problem is that not everyone is a team player. In companies with a strong sense of team spirit, you're going to feel like a loser for wanting to leave—or a traitor no longer to be trusted by anyone. Listen to this accountant who was formerly on staff at a utilities firm: "The perks were great, and the security I had was great. But I developed an insecurity within myself. I wanted to be out on my own, and I had a sense of disgust for staying. But everyone told me I was crazy for even thinking about quitting. What about the money? The prestige? It took a long time to leave and set up my own business, but when I finally did, I was extremely relieved."

Think about the tremendous pressure a single mate can exert

in trying to keep a spouse in an unhappy marriage. Then multiply that tenfold and you'll have an idea of the almost overwhelming pressure a team can exert on a member. The need for belonging can be terribly exploited; you just can't "desert" the team or "defect" to the competition. In the quest for approval, people might work way past their limits, destroying their physical and mental health, not to mention their personal life. I remember what one division manager at a large bank said: "This is the big leagues. If you want to play the game, this is the place to play it. No matter what it takes, we're going to be number one!"

How can you admit to your team members—and to yourself—that you want the minor leagues? Or the number ten slot in the play-offs?

You might not. Like the accountant at the utilities firm, you might persist, desperately trying to fit in. Understand that the downside of the New Maternalism is a team spirit intolerance for *anyone* who doesn't fit into the culture. Because a particular job or company is not right for you does not mean that you can't find a comfortable fit somewhere else where you can flourish and cheer with the best of them.

Knowing how your corporate family works is one way to make a "home sweet home" for yourself. The other is to analyze your needs, your fears, your aspirations—and the lies you tell yourself to stay in a bad situation.

In the next section, we'll zero in on *you*—not your family, not your team, and not the corporate home. I'll help you cut through the layers of delusion and illusion to find out what's *really* important to you in your corporate life and what—surprisingly—is not. . . .

Part 2

THE TIES THAT BIND

Chapter 5

The Lies That Bind

"There comes a point when your soul is owned by the company. You can no longer take the gamble. You're no longer free to leave."   —Owner, Personnel agency

In my fourteen years as a psychologist and career counselor, I have met hundreds of people who hated their jobs but never even looked around to see if they could find something better. In almost every case, the reasons for their unhappiness seemed obvious. People weren't inventing their own discomfort. Their problems were very real. What was far from obvious, however, was why they couldn't do anything constructive about the situation. Why were intelligent, resourceful, and even ambitious people getting stuck? Why couldn't they conduct an effective job search?

Slowly I began to see that while these people were telling me the absolute truth about their problems, they were telling themselves self-defeating lies about what could be done about them. In fact, I've distilled thirteen separate lies that kept coming up over and over again in my counseling sessions and in my interviews for this book. These are the rationalizations most of us, at one time or another, have used to convince ourselves we're doing the right thing to stay put. We might not be a part of that homogeneous happy family, but we'll close our eyes and pretend we can't change a thing.

It's easier to stay put—and what better way than to rationalize a bad situation, hanging on to the family we already have. In the words of one executive: "At least I know what I've got here."

This way of thinking comes with a very dear price tag: you. Your aspirations. Your needs. Your happiness. Examining these thirteen "lies that bind" will help you cut through the emotional clutter of your corporate family muddle. They'll help you see for yourself what is real—and what is not. But beware. They can be tricky. Each lie can very well be the bind that ties with false security. But each one is also potentially a statement of fact, an honest assessment of your job situation at this particular time.

If you find yourself saying any one of the following phrases, give yourself a personal true or false test. Evaluate them all and see if they're working for you—or against you.

Lie 1:

"IT WOULD BE DISLOYAL TO LOOK AROUND."

This is a fact: companies foster feelings of loyalty, and they are *not* going to like the idea of your looking around—unless they plan to fire you. Loyalty in good companies is rewarded and expected if you want to work your way up the ladder. But that same loyalty can turn into a lie that binds when it gets in the way of your personal happiness. Take the case of Joe, a successful financial analyst I interviewed. He'd grown up in a blue-collar family that had little money to send him to college. He received a partial scholarship to an Ivy League school, but the real funds for his education came from his part-time job at a prestigious investment house. When Joe was graduated, he joined the firm's full-time staff at a salary far beyond anything he ever dreamed he'd get. Their generosity generated real family feeling in him, motivating him to work extraordinary hours, literally twenty-four hours a day when the company needed it. But after a few years, the firm reorganized. "They took away the part of the job I liked most," Joe told me. "But I still put in the long hours. I didn't even think of looking around. I felt too much loyalty to the company." That loyalty was debilitating, ruining his health, his confidence, and ultimately his performance at work.

Joe was wrestling with guilt. After all, the company did pay for his education and took him on at a generous starting salary. When Joe took a long, hard look at his situation, however, he realized the guilt was misplaced. He'd already paid the company back many times over, not only with his long, industrious hours, but with his contribution to profits. The large bonus he received every year was based on his personal performance, the money *he* made for the company. In black and green, the bonus check proved that he was generating dollars for the company *while* earning his salary. The company was not in the charity business. He had earned his salary and bonuses.

If you're like Joe, staying on in a job gone sour because the company paid for your education or helped you through a financial or medical crisis, you might want to hang in there to pay it back—but *only* for a specified amount of time.

Reassess your guilt. If you don't want to leave that unfulfilling spot because the company or boss gave you training or promotions, think again. That's what a company *should* do for good workers. Your happiness and your career needs must come first. The next time you evaluate your loyalty to a corporation, figure out if you've already repaid your debt—in full. And ask yourself "Am I being loyal to myself?" instead.

Lie 2:

"I'M NEEDED."

Here's one dictum that's hard to believe but true: no one is indispensable. Remember the words of the manipulating Mighty Oz who tells his employees that he *needs* them, that they can't possibly leave him now. As an executive recruiter told me, "It's great for the ego to think the company will fall apart without you." But the plain fact is, it won't.

Julia, a client of mine, learned this the hard way. She worked as a salesperson for a chain of furniture stores, putting in forty-hour weeks but only earning five dollars an hour—with her lunch hour deducted. Since Julia desperately wanted to learn the business to become an interior designer, she kept at it. When her store's manager left, the chain's owner asked her to take on twenty more hours. They needed her. In fact, they needed her *so* much that she was soon doing the manager's job—hiring and firing, doing the books, training new salespeople—all for a raise of one dollar an hour. "My boss kept saying he needed me so much. He was so apologetic that he couldn't pay me more." The words *I'm needed* stuck in her brain even when Julia tallied the books and saw the store was netting $8,000 a month. She continued to push herself. One day she got sick, and her boss refused to get anyone to replace her. A coworker advised her, "Look, just shut the gate. It's not our store and it's not our responsibility." The message finally hit home. Julia gave notice and promptly found a company that appreciated her talent and hard work.

Julia was an extreme example, but I've seen many a savvy executive get hooked by this lie. If you ever find yourself saying "I'm needed," check out the facts before you accept it blindly. A company that really needs you will pay you commensurately, with a good salary and with benefits. If you're not getting the rewards for your "valuable position," it's time to think about leaving.

Lie 3:

"I MIGHT NOT HACK IT SOMEWHERE ELSE."

A brilliant lawyer with a Fortune 100 company believed this lie wholeheartedly even though he had been graduated with top honors from *two* Ivy League schools and had never received a less than excellent evaluation on the job. He'd been with his company for several years when he realized that even with his good salary and steady advancement, he was bored. He'd outgrown his position, but he refused to look around—not out of loyalty, but out of fear. "Job search is such a pain," he rationalized. "Besides, I know I can do the work here, and I'm not sure I can hack it somewhere else."

Or maybe this sounds familiar. Robert, a former golden boy, had a fifteen-year climb to the top that was beginning to slow down. The clincher came when someone else was given a top spot that had been slotted for him. Robert was furious, but he couldn't leave. "I can't imagine going out into the outside world. It's too strange. I've been out of circulation so long, I don't even know how to start."

Like Robert, if you're not doing well, paralysis can set in—your fear of uncharted territory compounded by a self-worth so low you can't believe anyone would want to hire you. This is rarely an accurate analysis. Poor performance is almost never a result of incompetence. It usually boils down to corporate culture clash or lack of enthusiasm.

How do you hack your way out of this debilitating lie? The answer is simple: do something to get out of your rut. Continue with your formal education if your skills are getting rusty. Make an active effort to keep up old contacts—or make new ones. Participate in business seminars to stay state-of-the-art. You'll not only perform better in your present job, but you'll have the confidence to face that strange new world head-on.

Lie 4:

"WHAT'S THE POINT OF LOOKING? I'LL ONLY BE DISAPPOINTED."

Only a total pessimist thinks it's bad all over. Unfortunately, there seem to be a lot of them around. Take the example of a communications expert I interviewed who told me he absolutely hates his job. "I have to design these telephone systems too fast, pushing them through and approving them even though I know they'll break down as soon as they're installed. Everyone feels the pressure; I'm not the only one. But the standard line is, if it's bad here, it'll just be worse somewhere else."

The reality is this: how do you really know how bad things are until you check it out? Looking does not mean leaving, and there's always the chance you'll find something good. Even if you decide to stay, your gloom should lighten. I've discovered that my most frustrated clients are those who've passively stayed put in unhappy situations. The clients who've taken *active* steps either to try to improve their jobs or to leave feel better. With all-out effort, most are able to make positive changes, but those who couldn't at least had the satisfaction of knowing they tried as hard as they could to help themselves. Research backs this up: studies show that once you make a definite decision to stay with a company, even one that's not completely satisfying, you'll feel better about your job. You've made an active choice, checking out all the alternatives, and have decided for yourself to stay.

Until you see what else is available, you'll hang your head in woe like the communications expert, neither in nor out, a victim of circumstance. Go out there. Find out. You don't want to be constantly churning. You just might uncover this lie for what it is: an excuse to keep you down.

Lie 5:

"I'VE INVESTED TOO MUCH TIME AND EFFORT TO LEAVE NOW."

Maybe. Maybe not. Prosperous Wall Street investors know that the two keys to success are 1) knowing when to stay with a winner and 2) knowing when to cut your losses. If you've invested a good deal of time and effort in a job where the odds of a payoff are slim, you'd better rethink this lie and find a home where your investment can have a more profitable return.

Easier said than done. The longer you are with a company, the harder it is to break free. You have become part of the family, and even if it is an unhappy family, you have a place in it—and that's hard to give up. In fact, any time you have invested enough time and effort to call "the" company, "my" company, leaving feels like a loss. That is understandable. You *will* lose your place in the company. But what is never lost is your experience and expertise. Those are assets you always take with you. I've known hundreds of people who turned loss into gain by changing jobs to find at least happier working conditions—and usually a move up the career ladder as well.

This lie can be valid, though, if leaving means a big pay cut or a real loss of security. An executive recruiter told me about a fifty-eight-year-old purchasing manager who'd come to see him after a new boss demoted him to a buyer slot. "I advised him to stay for seven years at his full salary until retirement. The company wouldn't fire him. At his age, he'd be risking too much to leave." If you do decide to settle in for the short run as this ex-purchasing manager ultimately did, make sure you don't become one of the "living dead" simply waiting for retirement. Do something challenging either on the job or outside the corporate walls to keep you vital.

If this lie has begun to weigh you down, invest some time and effort into a thorough examination of your situation. Whatever you decide, your investment will be solid.

Lie 6:

"I'LL WAIT UNTIL I HAVE MORE MONEY."

Get ready for a long, long wait. As Florida employment agency owner Virginia Vinson put it: "No one ever has enough money." Waiting for "enough" can just be a way of stalling. On the other hand, waiting for "more" can be valid protection against the unknown. Do a cost benefit analysis by asking yourself some realistic questions:

- How long do I have to stay to get more money?
- How much will I get if I wait?
- How much do I really need to maintain my life-style?
- Is waiting worth the psychological cost?
- Will the wait hurt my career?

A woman I know had only two years to go before she'd be fully vested in her company's profit sharing plan, able to walk away with $50,000. She felt the wait was worth it—even though she hated her job. But someone else might say, "Hey, that's two years out of my life. I'd rather go somewhere else and make up the $50,000 with better opportunities. I'd rather be free."

If you're staying on the job *just* for the money, it can be very demoralizing. Listen to this senior executive who walked away from a high six-figure salary: "I could have stayed and made a pile of money, but it was getting harder to cope. I had become a puppet. Just in it for the money. And then you're lost. You're basically castrated and you're living a sham."

No one wants to live a sham. Do what you can now; don't wait for tomorrow unless it makes good career sense. One man I interviewed, Bill, was a true procrastinator. He'd dreamed about becoming an entrepreneur for years, but he contined to stay at his banking job. Finally he went to an entrepreneurship seminar, and the words of the main speaker really hit home: "If you're past thirty-five and you keep saying you're going to start your own business, you probably won't do it." Bill was thirty-four and he took the message as a personal challenge. Within six months he'd started his own business . . . successfully.

Whenever you change jobs—and especially if you start your own business—it helps to have a financial cushion in case things don't work out and you wind up out on the street. A healthy nest egg or a working spouse can give you this "breathing room," as Dr. Marta Mooney, a business professor at Fordham University, found: men whose wives work full-time are three times more likely to consider changing jobs—and twice as likely to actually do it—as men married to homemakers.

Even if you're hesitant about the financial risks, check out all the alternative opportunities that come your way. You never know . . . dreams can come true. And *you* can make them happen.

Lie 7:

"THINGS ARE BAD, BUT THEY'LL NEVER FIRE ME."

Guess again. All you have to do is look at the business pages. Exxon. Atari. AT&T. The list goes on. Even companies that have rarely fired in the past have had major bloodlettings in the '80s. If they have to, companies *will* fire. Hiding your head in the out box is not going to change a thing.

Mike was one of those head-hiders who ignored the signs. "Profits were down for over a year. There was talk of cutting back to four days. But everybody was sure it was only a temporary setback. They wouldn't drop anyone. I was totally shocked when they let me go."

Though Mike was lulled into a false sense of security, some

people will stay with a troubled company knowing full well things are bad, and it can sometimes be a smart move. Consider the case of the chemical engineer who knew that his company was in deep trouble. No one was getting bonuses and business was bad. But he loved his job and he loved his company. He also had something more: realistic expectations. His decision was influenced by the fact that his sector of the chemical industry was in bad shape. He knew he wouldn't have much luck finding another job. He decided to stay.

The difference between this man and Mike comes down to choice. The engineer knew *exactly* what he was doing. He chose to stay after evaluating his other options. Mike chose to pretend nothing was wrong. Choosing will make all the difference to your world too.

Lie 8:

"A MOVE WILL BE BAD FOR MY FAMILY."

One executive recruiter takes a hard line about this particular lie: "When anyone says the wife doesn't like the location or the kids are in school, I don't buy it. That's just a rationalization. That just means they've plateaued out. They're afraid. When I hear this I assume this guy's hit the Peter Principle."

Maybe. But moving is a tricky issue. Other recruiters tell me that sometimes family ties *should* come before a career. Preferred location, a mate's career, or a child's attachment to school are often valid reasons to stay put, and these recruiters routinely see competent men and women turn down good jobs because of them.

The fact is that *any* move is disruptive, especially when a family is involved. It usually takes at least six months to feel at home in a new community, and some people never do. The impact of a move is especially difficult to assess if children are involved. Many parents fear their adolescents will suffer permanent emotional damage if uprooted. How can you know if this fear is valid? While some healthy children do suffer because of a move, in general, your child's past history of adjustment is the best predictor of the future. As Dr. Stephen Eliot, a Connecticut-based psychologist who specializes in working with corporate transferees, told me, "Kids who have serious problems after a move usually had problems before." On the positive side, Dr. Eliot notes that children who've moved two or three times while growing up seem to adjust better to college.

If you think this "lie" is gospel, think again. Make sure it's not your fear talking tongues. A friend of mine, for instance, didn't want to move to California when her husband was told to relocate. However, she realized he'd always resent her if she made him pass up this big promotion. She was terrified, but she took the plunge. "At forty-six," she said, "I decided I could use a change." Off she went. When she wrote me from her new California home, her first line was: "This place is paradise." As in good marriages, career paths are filled with compromise. You just have to know when and where to draw the line.

Unfortunately for some, there are no lines to draw. If you don't accept a relocation, your company might think you don't want to get ahead. It can kill your career. When one executive asked his boss if he had a choice, he got this reply: "You have every choice and no choice at all."

When that inner voice starts telling you a move will be hell on everyone, you might be wise to listen. But don't just accept this lie at face value. Watch out for rationalization. Examine all the facts *first*. You just might find, like my friend, that a move can be another view of paradise.

Lie 9:

"MAYBE THINGS WILL GET BETTER."

There's always the chance that policies might be reversed, bringing things back to the good ole way they used to be. Or that the bad boss might be moved to another department. And while we're at it, there's always the chance that profits will begin to soar again soon.

But there's always the chance that things will get worse instead. You have to be realistic. Are you continuing to ignore the cold, hard truth—or is there really a good possibility for an upward swing? A real estate developer I interviewed decided to hang in there when a new firm with deep pockets acquired his troubled company. "They had lots of money," he told me, "but they managed my firm as if they didn't. After four years of waiting for things to get better, nothing happened. I had to take a hard look at the probability of change and set a time limit."

Like this developer, we don't always like to face up to things. But if we don't, we can waste a lot of years in fruitless hope.

Lie 10:

"THERE'S A NEW REGIME, BUT THINGS WILL STAY EXACTLY THE SAME."

Don't believe it for a second. While you're sitting behind your desk, pleased as punch and filling out your latest expense account, plans are being hatched in the big corner office down the hall. Most of the managers I interviewed for this book said that the first thing they did when they took over a company or department was call a meeting to reassure the staff, all the while making their plans for changes. It's not a question of ethics. It's a fact of business life. The easiest way for managers to make their mark in a new company is to bring in their own people and start fresh. You can be fired because of a chemistry clash. Because you look too young. Too old. Too different. Too much of a threat. Or too much deadwood.

How to avoid a possible purge? Face up to the facts. Update your résumé. Keep your contacts and your confidence so if you do have to leave, you'll be able to cope.

To increase the odds in your favor, join the new regime. Become "invaluable" to your new boss. Help. Go out of your way. Do it the way he or she likes without hostility. But don't sell your soul. Then you're not only thinking a lie, but living it.

Lie 11:

"I'M NOT HAPPY, SO SOMETHING MUST BE WRONG WITH ME."

Probably not. This particular breed of lie is nourished in people who work for very prestigious companies. I remember an executive who worked for a Fortune 100 company confiding that he was miserable. He constantly asked himself, "What's wrong with me? I'm with one of the best companies in the world, and I'm not happy." With careful analysis, he was finally able to pinpoint the problem. It wasn't that anything was wrong with him. He was a seat-of-the-pants decision maker working for a company where memo-writing was an art. He left his Fortune 100 firm and found a new niche in a smaller company that was more informal. "I love the fact that the decisions are made so fast here," he told me recently. "We rarely write memos."

Remember the old cliché: "Different strokes for different folks." You won't just find this lie germinating in prestigious corporations. You'll find it born and bred at home. Maybe your father or mother flourished in the legal profession and you feel you *have* to do well as a lawyer too. Or maybe they always dreamed you'd become a doctor—even though you hate the sight of blood. Maybe your friends, family, and everyone you work with thinks your company is one of "The 100 Best Companies to Work for in America." Fine for them. Whenever this lie creeps up, look to *your* opinions and personality before you decide so quickly, "It's all my fault."

Lie 12:

"IF I CAN'T DO THIS, I CAN'T DO ANYTHING."

No, no, no. If you're not doing well, it's most likely because you're in the wrong field, with the wrong boss, or in the wrong company. It usually has nothing to do with your ability. I've discovered that my clients who found settings better suited to their style also found more success. But first they had to stop feeling as if they had failed.

John, a forty-year-old businessman, had a part-time job cutting cheese for S. S. Pierce in Boston when he was nineteen. He hated it and was, consequently, inept. He was ultimately fired because he kept cutting his finger and bleeding all over the cheese. Of course, being bad at cutting cheese simply means he was bad at cutting cheese. Period. But John generalized his failure. He decided he couldn't do anything right and went through a depression that lasted for years. Happily, John's now a successful executive who's escaped the bind of this lie. With his new perspective, John has become a department head in a volatile record company, handling all the "big cheeses" without a single mishap.

Lie 13:

"ANY MOVE WOULD BE A STEP DOWN."

Could be. If working for the "top" firm is important to you, then this lie becomes truth. Then again, you may have no problem going to a smaller company where you'll get more pay or better benefits—even if no one has ever heard of the place.

It does stroke the old ego when people are impressed by your corporate home address. In some circles, it's simply expected. A Harvard M.B.A. recently went to a reunion and discovered that anyone not working at the "right" places was considered at best strange—and at worst a failure. But as with all the other "lies that bind," truth is in the eyes of the beholder—you. What are your goals? What do you want? What are your values on the job? How willing are you to trade off the ability to drop the "right" name of your employer for the opportunity to have a job you like more? By analyzing such questions, you can clear away the self-defeating lies that tie you down and help you get to the truth.

So does analyzing the smorgasbord of tempting psychological and financial benefits companies offer their people. These benefits can foster the thirteen "lies that bind," or they can keep you a happy member of the family tree.

I'll be examining these temptations next, digging deeper into the truth behind what you *want* versus what you *have* in your present corporate home. . . .

Chapter 6

Golden Handcuffs and Key Benefits

"He'd love my income with his security, and I'd love the hours of his job with *my* income. Unfortunately, it just doesn't work that way. You have to make trade-offs."

—Director of marketing,
Manufacturing firm

Golden Handcuffs are not Tiffany jewelry for the S&M market. Golden Handcuffs is personnel jargon for financial perks that lock employees to a job: the dangling "phantom" stock, the deferred payments, the stock options or vested partnerships that are ours if we just hang in there for three, five, or fifteen years. They are downright manipulative, appealing to the darker, greedier side of our personalities—and they work.

Golden Handcuffs are only a small part of the benefits story. Every job offers assets, golden or otherwise, that can lure us in and keep us going—either out of contentment or fear of loss. Any of those psychological and financial benefits a company can offer—from prestige to free time, from great location to challenge—might handcuff us to a job for better or worse, richer or poorer, 'til retirement do you part. . . .

The question is whether the benefits you are getting are the ones you really want—and whether you could get them elsewhere. As with the other attachments to our corporate family, we may be only partially aware of how the various handcuffs trap us. Without careful analysis we might never know what it is we want. In fact, industrial psychologists have been grappling with that question for years.

I think the answer is clear: different people want different things at different times in their lives. For example, young singles might gravitate to the companies that offer training and challenge, but as they get older, good medical, dental, and retirement plans become a real plus. The quest for power might completely obsess a person at age forty but become meaningless at fifty; the person in the next office could flip-flop the opposite way.

I've already explored the lies we tell ourselves to keep what we have. Now it's time to separate what we have from what we want. The best way to differentiate our individual "haves" from our "have-nots" is to examine each Handcuff, one by one, to see which of them hits home. Once you know what's important to you and what is not, it should become clear whether you're getting what you want from your present job or unhappily settling into a lie that binds.

All forty Handcuffs are here, in black and white, mapped out in seven basic benefit categories:

- The Quality of the Organization
- The Work Environment
- Money
- Growth
- Interpersonal Relations
- Life-style
- Job Content

Be honest with yourself as you look over each Handcuff. Everyone has his own "most wanted" list. Different companies offer different goodies to attract the kinds of people *they* want.

To have a happy home, your needs and the company's offerings have to fit.

Don't be surprised if some of the Handcuffs seem like direct contradictions. They are. It's impossible to seek out all forty. We constantly have to make trade-offs and compromises to get what we want from our jobs. If you want a job that stops promptly at five, you'll probably have to forego the dream of earning mega-bucks. If you need the security of a job, you might have to sacrifice challenge.

Skim through this chapter first so you won't get overwhelmed trying to juggle all forty benefits in your head. After you get this overview of Benefitsland, I'll give you an easy method for specif-ically sorting out what you most want—your Key Benefits List—and what you can take or leave. Stimulation or security? Less hours or more money? What's the combination that makes you tick? Read on. . . .

Benefits Category 1:

THE QUALITY OF THE ORGANIZATION

Maybe your key benefit is benefiting others. Or perhaps it's cru-cial for you to be a part of an organization that's fair and honest, or simply prestigious. If so, you'll find part of your Key Benefits List combination here.

1. *Ethics and Values*
It feels good working for a company that cares about the quality of its products and services, where employees don't have to com-promise their integrity. For one Procter & Gamble executive, it's an important benefit: "There's a lot of integrity here. We want the *best* product in every category. We pulled Rely tampons off the market at the first hint there'd be a problem to the consumer —long before we had to. Other companies wouldn't have done that. I feel proud working for P&G."

2. Altruism

People who want to make the world a better place usually find their place in a nonprofit organization. Unfortunately, altruists often have to trade-off the comparatively high salaries and perks that corporate life offers if they switch to the nonprofit world. The alternative is to be altruistic in your off-hours, or to work for many of the good corporations that make a profit *and* do something for the public at large. Two such firms are Oneida, which considers the impact that corporate decisions will have on the community, and H. B. Fuller, which encourages its employees' volunteer activities and contributes heavily to charity.

3. Prestige

Some people need the name. They'd be embarrassed if no one heard of their firm or product. It makes people feel proud, for instance, to say that they work for General Mills instead of some unknown food manufacturer that turns out private label brands. Plus well-known company names can open doors. As a newspaper reporter in Michigan told me: "If I were a free-lancer and tried to get a quote from the mayor, who knows when my calls would be returned. But when I say I'm from *The Detroit News,* they get back to me that day."

Benefits Category 2:

THE WORK ENVIRONMENT

These benefits derive from the way your firm does business. Do you get to work on your own? Do you need and receive a lot of direction? Do you know the ropes? Do the company's policies feel right?

4. Entrepreneurial Possibilities

This is important for free spirits—or people who simply want a piece of the pie. In Silicon Valley computer experts routinely leave secure jobs to help start up new firms, knowing full well that they'll have to invest two or three years of sixty- and seventy-hour weeks in a company that could fail. Why? For the chance to become part owner of a future success. Computer technology is not the only field that offers entrepreneurial spice. Real estate development firms often give their employees a piece of each deal. Commissions give salespeople a direct benefit from what they've put in.

5. Surroundings

Some people can't stand a company with a low-overhead philosophy. They have to work in a beautiful building or have an attractive office, and what furnishes that office can be an important symbol of success. A friend of mine once chose a sleek office desk instead of a pay increase. Many managers would feel uncomfortable without an impressive view. At the new American Express headquarters, top executives will get the latest ultimate status symbol: a fireplace.

6. Support Staff and Facilities

In a bold headline, a recent advertisement in *The New York Times* asked, "Why don't more lawyers go out on their own?" It was answered in the body copy: "Because they have to pay to get what they want. Simple things like an office. A secretary. Typewriters . . ." The list went on. For some people, having good backup services is extremely important. As a successful literary agent told me: "I was divorced three times. Each time it was upsetting. But I didn't really know what upset was until I divorced my publishing house. It was awful. Husbands provide a lot, but a publishing house provides messenger service!"

7. Direction

There are those who need to know what's good and what's bad and have it spelled out by their firm. Others flee from formal policy like the plague, like this young manager at Sony: "It's informally run with very few policies and procedures. It's not hierarchical. People can pursue their own ideas." When it comes to finding a simpatico corporate culture, knowing how much—or how little—direction you like can help point you in the right "direction."

8. Structure

Some people need a routine day in and day out. One man who left a large firm to start his own business said, "The hardest thing was to get structure in my life. At my big corporation the calendar year was laid out for me. I knew what I was going to do every single day. Many days now I just don't know what to do. It takes a lot of getting used to."

The literary agent who missed her messengers couldn't afford a secretary when she started out on her own. She hired one anyway to give a structure to her days. When the secretary arrived at nine o'clock, she couldn't be caught dawdling over the papers. She *had* to be dressed and ready to go.

9. Feedback

Most people agree that a good manager gives plenty of feedback. It helps trainees learn, and it eliminates the uncomfortable ambiguity even top managers feel when no one comments on their performance. As one senior vice-president told me, "I like to know how I'm doing. If the client or the president tells me he is pleased, it makes me feel good. If they tell me there's a problem, at least I know where I stand."

10. Knowing the Ropes

Search firm owner Peter Grimm says, "Leaving a job is like leaving the womb. You always get surprises." Surprises mean risks. There's a real comfort in knowing all the ins and outs of a company's culture. As a manager in the jewelry manufacturing business told me, "I know who counts and what counts and how to get things done here." He'd never leave it.

73

Benefits Category 3:

MONEY

Maybe you work only for the money. Maybe you think that's selling out. Regardless, research shows that money is the prime motivator. Take a look at the following benefits and see if any of them are "on the money."

11. Income

To be satisfied, people have to have an income that provides at least the minimal life-style they want. It also has to be "fair": most people have to get paid what their friends are getting paid in similar jobs, and they have to get paid what they feel they're worth. People will switch jobs for more money, but what they'll get depends on the economy and inflation rates. During the big inflation of the 1970s, a 35 percent increase in pay was not unusual. In 1955 that figure was only 10 percent. Right now the typical pay increase is between 7 and 15 percent, or double the inflation rate. If you're tempted to switch jobs for an increase, beware. Research shows that on average those who stay with a company long-term end up with higher salaries than those who hop for a raise.

12. Wealth

Several recruiters mentioned that the higher an employee is on the career ladder, the harder it is to get him to switch jobs merely for more income. But if that top employee is motivated by money, he or she may be lured by "wealth." What's the difference between income and wealth? Well, if you have to ask, you probably don't have it. Income, even fat six-figure incomes, are eaten up by taxes and living expenses. Wealth is a separate pile of money above your normal living expenses that you can sock away. Wealth is the big lump of a bonus, the Golden Handcuff, or the piece-of-the-pie program that can make you "instantly" rich.

13. Benefit Plans

An executive I know wrote down all the pros and cons of a new job offer before accepting: "The dental plan was a real pro. With three kids, I had to think about this. Ten years ago, I never would have cared." Whether or not you care, if you work for a large company, much of your compensation is in unseen benefits. A study done at Merck Drugs showed that one quarter to one third of people's salaries are in benefits. If someone is earning $34,000 a year, they have an additional $8,000 in benefits. "Benefit levels have gotten so good at so many companies that it's almost a given," a personnel manager at a Fortune 500 company explained. "Any prestigious company would have a very hard time attracting people without a big benefits package. It's just expected."

14. Perks

It's great to get something for free. At Wang, there's a free country club. The airlines give free travel. At *Reader's Digest,* employees are reimbursed for any kind of self-improvement course. At AT&T, people get $35.00 worth of free long-distance phone calls a month. But employees have to look at their company's tax-advantaged perks with a realistic eye. The IRS is getting more and more interested in taxing perks. And with a job change that nets a $5,000–$10,000 raise, a person could buy the country club membership and travel as well. But for some, it just wouldn't feel the same.

15. Security

Like any catchword, security means something different to everybody, but it can be all-important for those who want peace of mind. It's almost impossible to fire civil servants. Teachers strive for tenure. And corporations with a reputation for job security can sound like safe havens. But there's a danger inherent in security as well: it can be the most psychologically binding benefit of them all. Roger Myers, a psychology professor at Columbia University's Teachers College, has studied a number of people who stayed in jobs solely because of security. "Retirement and security can become a superordinate goal that permits eating a lot of humble pie. It's a career strategy, but it's not at all fulfilling." Not fulfilling, but necessary for some. A search professional with the large Management Recruiters organization explained, "Security is so important for some people that if they went to a new place where there wasn't any, they'd create their own havoc." At a time when corporate America is firing more and regretting it less, perhaps the greatest security is found at places like J. C. Penney, where the culture values loyalty and where they promote from within.

Benefits Category 4:

GROWTH

Your career path up the ladder—how concerned are you about getting ahead? Enough to leave your present job? Maybe moving up the ladder fast is the prime hook on your Key Benefits List. Or maybe you like your growth sure and steady, one step at a time.

16. *Upward Mobility*

If Upward Mobility is your number one, you're not alone. Executive recruiters say it's more powerfully motivating than money when it comes to switching jobs. Tucson-based executive search firm owner John Mezzapelle told me about a man who was with a corporation in Texas, working for a boss who was only two years older than himself. "He correctly assumed his boss would stay another twenty years, blocking him from any upward mobility. So he switched jobs with no salary increase but with the promise that if he did well, he'd receive a large promotion in a couple of years." Those interested in Upward Mobility have to look not only at their job, but at their department as well. A high-level manager I interviewed said, "In any corporation there's a line to the top. In a consumer products company, it's the marketing department. In an ad agency, it's account work or creative. In many other places, it helps if you're in finance." In summary, those who want to move up must look at the different levels of management above them and answer the following questions: Did most of top management come from a background like yours? Is your boss creating a permanent block or a smooth upward draft?

17. Training/Learning

Many people need good training to feel competent and to provide credentials and skills that give them mobility. Even within the same industry, firms vary widely in the amount of training they provide. The ad agency Young & Rubicam is famous for its extensive training programs. Other agencies provide none. They'll either lure trained people away from the competition or establish a sink-or-swim environment where you're expected to get the training on your own.

18. State-of-the-Art Experience

It's important for some to be up on the newest technologies and advancements in their field. A headhunter for Silicon Valley says, "People here have enormous security because they believe in their capabilities. Anyone good can get a job or start a company. Job security is not an issue because knowledge of the technology provides internal confidence." Managers who crave this benefit should make sure that the state of their job isn't so administrative that they lose touch.

19. Visibility

Everybody likes to be noticed, especially those who realize it's a real key to career advancement. They'll find their niche in positions that allow them to interact with top management. One industrial psychologist advises managers to give ambitious employees a special assignment reporting to the CEO if they can't dole out a raise or promotion. "That gives them the impression that they are on the move . . . that they would be foolish to leave the firm because they are getting closer and closer to the president."

Benefits Category 5:

INTERPERSONAL RELATIONS

Some of us will sacrifice Upward Mobility for a sense of belonging. It's a feeling that money can't buy.

20. Being Known/Positive Identity within the Organization

As one man said, "I'm known as good old George. And good old George does a fine job. That's a real ego boost for me, and I wouldn't want to lose it." Many people need to be a good old George.

21. Family Attachment

Many companies like to keep things *all* in the family, and they'll actively encourage employees' mates and children to join in on the parties and after-work activities. This "togetherness" feels stifling for some, but it spells happiness for others. Then there are people who want to continue a real family tradition. Whether it's following a long line of stockbrokers, doctors, or one-company men, they'll stay where they are even if they're not content. An accountant I spoke to in a large accounting firm didn't like his work. But he came from a family where everyone was an accountant, and his father had always wanted him to join one of the "Big Eight." "He is so proud of me, telling all his friends about his son who really made it in New York. What would he think if I left?"

22. *Supervisory Relations*

Some people could never work for a Mommie Dearest boss or a Generalissimo or any boss they just didn't like—even if it could benefit their career. And working for a Superboss can be a real plus: it not only makes life pleasant, but it also paves a career path. Many managers follow their mentors to the top.

23. *Associates*

Remember the powerful emotional bonds built up between siblings in the corporate home? For some, it's a benefit they won't want to give up. A woman I know was offered a job in a cutthroat corporation and turned it down. "I could have made more money," she told me, "but I'd have to give up the quality of the environment I have now. I like the people here. There's a minimum of politics and good work gets rewarded. I don't want to leave that."

24. *Social Involvement*

While some people deliberately keep their work and personal life separate, others have built up a whole social scene around their office friends. They'll shine in corporations where employees gather at the company cafeteria, the local bar, or at after-work parties. Transferring to a less friendly place would feel like a stint in Siberia.

25. *Team Spirit*

I've already discussed the pros and cons of the new team spirit found in corporations today. If it's a solid connection, it can feel absolutely right.

Benefits Category 6:

LIFE-STYLE

Many executive recruiters and personnel managers find this category unnerving. They can't understand this group of benefits because its importance lies outside the corporate walls. An outgrowth of the humanistic movement of the 1960s and '70s, the focus on life-style is a relatively new phenomenon that stresses the value of life away from the corporate family circle.

26. Free Time

Teachers consider free time so important that they shun corporate jobs with long hours and short vacations. As a group, secretaries often sacrifice Upward Mobility and higher income for the freedom of working "only" 9 to 5. And the secret benefit for many out-of-the-office salespeople is that few ever work five eight-hour days a week.

27. Personal Style

This benefit's lure is more tempting to creative people than administrators. A friend of mine always wore a vivid yellow blouse for interviews—even though her employment agency warned her it wasn't conservative enough. "I knew if I was offered the job in spite of my favorite yellow blouse, it would be a place I'd want to work for."

28. Family Life

For those with a strong family bond, a job that gives them lots of time to spend at home is a real plus. Since so many people feel torn between their obligations at work versus home, I've devoted an entire chapter to this topic later on.

29. Location

Some people may want to live near Denver for the skiing. Others might pick the Carolinas for the beaches. Still others can be like the man who lived in a nondescript Midwestern town who told me, "I'd leave my job in a minute, but I refuse to leave my community. I love it too much."

Benefits Category 7:

JOB CONTENT

These are the intrinsic values we look for in a job, the hooks that appeal to our inherent nature. They can increase our satisfaction and pleasure—or destroy our self-worth. How important is the job's challenge to you? Can you be creative enough? Do you have a real need to achieve? And power . . . how much do you crave?

30. Power
Some search firms won't even talk to anyone who doesn't want it. As one high-level search firm owner said: "People make a change to find power and move ahead. Everybody I place wants to be president." Talking to a headhunter like this can make you believe that anyone who doesn't lust after power is a wimp. On the other hand, talking to proponents of a laid-back life-style can make you believe that anyone who craves power is neurotic. Obviously the truth about power, like all the other benefits, lies within you. It is simply a matter of personal choice. The research on whether or not power corrupts confirms this: power can be handled in a very healthy manner. It's the people who want power but don't have it (especially over their own lives) who develop the biggest problems.

31. Responsibility
Some people like lots—and they'll flock to the jobs that put them on the line. Others cave in from too much responsibility. They'll spell this benefit S-T-R-E-S-S.

32. Challenge

Like all these Job Content benefits, Challenge can work both ways. It can be an exhilarating hook or a self-defeating trap. For some people it's all-important. Why else would Felix Rohatyn leave his powerful, high-paying position as partner of a major investment banking firm to straighten out New York City's financial mess—for one dollar a year? I talked to many people who happily traded income or security for "a real challenge." At the top executive levels, stratospheric salaries are often not prized as money, but as markers of how well a challenge was met.

33. Creativity

In their best-selling book, *In Search of Excellence,* authors Thomas J. Peters and Robert H. Waterman, Jr., define excellence as "continuously innovative big companies" that encourage their employees to run with their ideas. Creativity is a basic need for good business—and *the* basic need for some business people. One of my clients had gone so far up the ladder in his architectural firm that he was doing administrative work instead of designing. "I'd risen beyond a point where I could use my creativity the way I like." He ultimately changed the function of his position so he could still "get his hands dirty."

34. Achievement

Accomplishment was so important to heart surgeon Dr. William DeVries that he used to raise the money himself to perform his transplants. Humana Hospital successfully recruited him by telling him they would supply the money so he'd be free to operate. At Prudential Bache and other large stock brokerage houses, top-selling "superbrokers" are not "burdened" by managerial duties, and they have whole technical support systems geared just for them. In many firms, people work hard for bonuses or prizes, not only for their value but as symbols of achievement.

35. Independence

Some people define it as being able to set their own hours. Others take it to mean they can make their own decisions or rules. However it's construed, Independence is not usually found in large supply in corporations below the top levels. Free-lancing and consulting are good job alternatives for those who love its taste.

36. Importance

Everyone wants to feel that his or her job has worth. No one can be happy just shuffling papers. Perhaps you don't have to believe that things will completely fall apart without you, but you may want to feel that you are making a highly significant contribution to peoples' lives or to the corporate good. This feeling can come from a variety of jobs. Some people find keeping the corporate books tedious drudgery. In the same role, others will be filled with importance.

37. Variety

Many people find it the spice of life. One of the most repeated complaints I heard during my interviews for this book was: "I couldn't stand sitting behind a desk doing the same thing day in and day out." Variety is one of the reasons why many managers like their jobs; there's an infinite number of different issues and decisions to be made each day. Variety lured one of the men I interviewed from a large, prestigious corporation to a smaller firm. "I love working here," he subsequently told me. "I have to do everything from negotiating the leases for the offices to entertaining the clients to coming up with a marketing plan."

38. Pace

Some people like to walk fast and get three things done at once. They like the urgency, the competitive edge. Others prefer a more peaceful and stately routine. Whichever rhythm feels right, it can be the hook "with legs" for many.

39. Prestige of the Job or Title

There are those who wouldn't trade their vice-presidential title at one place for more money at another. Position strokes the ego and has its social benefits. As one woman told me, "Being a television producer is a large part of my identity. It says I'm an important person. I'm doing something exciting. I say it at a cocktail party and people want to talk to me. If I tell them I'm a homemaker, they drift away."

40. Fun or Enjoyment of the Task

"Work is so much more fun than fun. It's improperly called work." That's Trammell Crowe, a self-made Texas billionaire, talking. And he's right. In order to be extremely successful, people have to do something they love to do. They'll automatically devote more time and energy to it—and do a better job.

Picking from the whole smorgasbord of benefits can be confusing, especially when you have to keep turning the pages back and forth. I promised you an easy method to discover your Key Benefits List in the beginning of this chapter. Take forty index cards. Write each benefit (listed on the following pages) on a separate card. This gives you a tangible way to sort out which are important to you and which are not—a very physical way to sort out priorities. Shuffle them around. See how you feel about each one. I'll give you more specific ways to use your cards in the following section, Moving On, where you'll find the necessary nuts and bolts for building a case to stay happily in your corporate home or to divorce your corporation in the least traumatic way.

BENEFITS LIST
WITH EXPLANATIONS

- **ETHICS AND VALUES**
My company is fair, honest, and reputable in its dealings with customers and employees. It cares about the quality of its products and services.

- **ALTRUISM**
My organization benefits people or society and/or makes the world a better place.

- **PRESTIGE OF THE ORGANIZATION**
People are impressed by my company. It has a strong, positive reputation and is respected.

- **ENTREPRENEURIAL POSSIBILITIES**
My organization allows me to run a piece of business as if it were my own and/or my company is open to letting me develop my own new business projects.

- **SURROUNDINGS**
I work in an attractive place with plenty of amenities. There is space and light, and furnishings are good-looking.

- **SUPPORT STAFF AND FACILITIES**
I have access to all the equipment and supplies I need to do a good job. There is enough staff and they are trained and available to help me in my endeavors.

- **DIRECTION**
The goals, policies, procedures, and hierarchy are either as formal or informal as I like. Management is available to give assistance and clarification in the manner I like.

- **STRUCTURE**
I like the fact that my company provides a place to go each day. The calendar year is laid out for me and my hours are filled with work.

- **FEEDBACK**
I know how I stand and how my work is being received. I am told if I'm not meeting objectives. I am praised when my work is good.

- **KNOWING THE ROPES**
I know how to get things done and who to go to if I need help. I feel comfortable because I know my job and the organization well.

- **INCOME**
I am well paid and/or earn enough to have most of the things I want.

- **WEALTH**
Golden Handcuffs—stock options or other programs—are in place to provide me with future wealth.

BENEFITS LIST
WITH EXPLANATIONS

- **BENEFIT PLANS**
I have good medical, insurance, retirement, and dental plans.

- **PERKS**
I have a company car, expense account, or other goodies.

- **SECURITY**
I have all reasonable assurance of a steady income and regular employment.

- **UPWARD MOBILITY**
There is clear opportunity for advancement at my company and/or the work I am doing will allow me to leave my firm and advance my status elsewhere. My department provides a clear path to the top.

- **TRAINING/ LEARNING**
My company or job helps me learn more and expand my skills.

- **STATE-OF-THE-ART EXPERIENCE**
I am up on the newest discoveries in my field. I am working with the latest and best equipment, ideas, and/or some of the best minds.

- **VISIBILITY**
My department is profitable, growing, and noticed by top management. I am given assignments that make me known to the company leaders.

- **BEING KNOWN/ POSITIVE IDENTITY WITHIN THE ORGANIZATION**
People say hello to me wherever I go within my organization. I am well known and well liked.

- **FAMILY ATTACHMENTS**
My mate or family is very involved with my work and/or my company. My family has very strong, positive feelings about it.

- **SUPERVISORY RELATIONS**
My supervisor and/or higher management in the company is fair, knowledgeable, and positive about me.

- **ASSOCIATES**
I enjoy working with the people in my organization. I like them and respect them. On the whole, relationships among the people in my company are good.

- **SOCIAL INVOLVEMENT**
Work gives me companionship that extends beyond business. I am invited to go out to lunch or to do things after hours.

- **TEAM SPIRIT**
People within my department work well together and help each other out. The different departments within my company

are cooperative. Politics are not at an unproductive level.

• **FREE TIME**
I have enough free time for my personal interests during the week and/or for vacations.

• **PERSONAL STYLE**
My work permits me to live my own unique way or to be my own unique self.

• **FAMILY LIFE**
My work does not interfere with the needs of my family.

• **LOCATION**
Work is near my family, friends, or recreational areas. There is an appealing climate and/or a pleasant commute from my home.

• **POWER**
I am in charge of people and procedures. I can do things such as hire, fire, set policies, or order the equipment I need. If there are leaders above me, I have influence with them.

• **RESPONSIBILITY**
I am as accountable as I like for my work. I get the right amount of supervision, the right amount of credit, and the right amount of autonomy for solving problems that crop up.

• **CHALLENGE**
I can take on difficult tasks and overcome interesting problems.

• **CREATIVITY**
I am encouraged or allowed to develop new ideas. I can invent or design new things, procedures, or concepts.

• **ACHIEVEMENT**
Work gives me a feeling of accomplishment.

• **INDEPENDENCE**
I can do things my own way and be on my own as much as I want.

• **IMPORTANCE**
I believe what I am doing is meaningful and makes a contribution to my firm.

• **VARIETY**
My work is not all the same all the time. I get to do different things or go different places.

• **PACE**
The pace suits me. It is as hectic or as leisurely as I like.

• **PRESTIGE OF THE JOB OR TITLE**
My work or title is impressive to other people. It engenders respect within and/or outside my organization.

• **FUN OR ENJOYMENT OF THE TASK**
I like what I do. I might even be tempted to do it if I didn't get paid.

Part 3

MOVING ON

Chapter 7

Knowing When It's
Time to Go

"You can't just push a button and abort a career."
—Senior manager,
Service organization

When I think of someone being happy in a job, I remember the words of an account executive in an advertising agency: "Every time I walk into my building, I say, 'How am I going to have a good time today?'"

Unfortunately, many of us are asking less gratifying questions when we push our way through the office doors. One man I interviewed felt frustrated every time he sat down at his desk: "You can do an outstanding job or a poor job. It doesn't make any difference paywise. The only merit system around here says the more competent you are, the more they dump on you." He's staying, but only for retirement benefits—and it's obviously ripping him up inside.

Then there's the manager whose career isn't progressing. He keeps asking himself, "Why am I unhappy?" but his debilitating fears prevent him from finding any answers or acting on his unhappiness.

Changing jobs is tricky. One researcher found 80 percent of all employees who leave their old home for a new one think they're leaving for a better job. He discovered, however, that only half of the moves really involved promotions. Self-delusion and recruiting "puffery" ran rampant. Obviously, change involves risk and new jobs are difficult to assess, but those are chances you might have to take if your happiness and success are at stake. Often, though, it's just not worth the risk.

What about you? Is it worth waiting for a future payoff, or should you be going for more money now? Is it worth the risk to plunge into a high-paying job that's essentially a sink-or-swim situation fraught with sharks? Are you getting what you want out of your job? Are you, like the account executive, having a good time in your corporate home right now? Or, like the unhappy manager, should you be moving on?

Management consultant Dan Adams put it succinctly: "Some people quit and leave. Others quit and stay." I've added another thought: "Still others stay and grow."

It all comes down to choice—even though it might look as if there's no choice at all. It's hard to know if moving on to a new job is the right decision. When you're busy juggling day-to-day responsibilities, it's easier to put your personal career plans on a back burner. On the other hand, the excitement of the "road" may have you packing a bag before you're really ready, hopping from a job filled with potential to one that will leave you trapped.

One thing is certain. Any time you're unhappy in your job, it's *always* a cue to move on, either to another company, to another position within your current home, or to a more positive way of handling your present situation.

Whichever route you decide to take, it must be the result of clearheaded thinking. Then you can do what's right for you with a minimum of pain.

By this time, you should have a better understanding of your corporate family roots and your role as a member of the team. You're ready to assess your own situation, accurately weighing your personal list of pros and cons to see if you're getting what you need and what you want. The Ties That Bind section helped steer you in the right direction. This section will get you moving, best foot forward.

To leave or not to leave. That is the question. Let's move on and discover *your* answer. . . .

INFORMATION, PLEASE

In knowledge there is strength. The accuracy of your personal "leave or stay equation" will depend on your understanding of the facts. You'll find the facts inside yourself—your feelings, aspirations, and delusions—and outside, where information about your career comes from corporate policy, politics, and temperament.

Before you can figure out how the external variables affect your situation, you have to understand the things that make you tick. So starting from the inside out, let's begin your leave or stay analysis with four basic questions that will help you know yourself:

"HOW DO YOU FEEL?"

Do you have trouble getting out of bed? Does the prospect of a whole day at your job get you down? Do you do a lot of daydreaming at your desk? Do you fantasize that things will get better? These are all early warning signs that something is wrong. By bringing these thoughts into sharper focus, you'll be able to pinpoint where your unhappiness lies and, more importantly, begin to assess if your situation can change. One executive who was working under a particularly critical top management team kept wishing that his superiors' personalities would magically change—or they'd drop dead. By taking his fantasy seriously, he understood how severe the personality conflicts with top management were. He also realized that they were not going to change and neither would he. Since they ran the company, he sadly came to grips with the fact that there was no place to go but out. He was then able to direct his energy away from angry daydreams and toward a positive job search.

"WHAT DO YOU WANT?"

This is where the benefit cards will come in handy. Sort them into three separate piles: *Very Important, Moderately Important,* and *Not Important.* Then pick out the top six benefits in your *Very Important* pile. This is your Key Benefits List: the criteria with which all job options can be evaluated. Can you get these six things in your current position—or anywhere in the company? It might sound like child's play, but I've discovered that seeing what you want in black and white will tell you immediately if you're getting it in your present corporate home . . . or if you'll have to leave to be fulfilled. Listen to these Key Benefits List success stories.

A woman deeply involved in corporate life had been given a good job offer, a risky but challenging chance to become a partner in an entrepreneurial enterprise. Her husband and her parents wanted her to stay where she was, as a secure, successful (but somewhat stultified) middle manager in a highly structured Fortune 100 company. After sorting through her cards, she discovered that "Challenge" and "Fun" were her highest priorities, and "Security" and "Family Attachments" were all-time lows. Her Key Benefits List cards showed in concrete terms that she should opt for the entrepreneurial offer. She did—and I'm pleased to report that she's not only doing extremely well with each new challenge that comes her way, but she's having a whole lot of fun as well.

Another man had two conflicting benefits on his list: "Knowing the Ropes" and "Challenge." On careful analysis, he realized he could have both if he stayed at his job—where he knew the procedures and the people ("Knowing the Ropes") —but stretched himself by asking for new assignments ("Challenge") inside the corporate family.

You can use these cards to examine almost any corporate situation. For instance, if "Ethics and Values" and "Altruism" find their way into your *Important* pile, while "Income" is decidedly *Not Important,* you may be better off in a nonprofit organization than a business. Study your cards. They can go a long way to help predict whether you can be happy where you are.

"WHAT DID YOU WANT?"

The first two questions deal with your present. This one is all about your past. Have your needs changed? Are you disillusioned? As one manager told me: "People get stuck in jobs because they forget what they wanted in the first place." To get as much as you can from this question, you might want to go back to your cards and pick out the benefits that were most important to you when you first joined the company. What did you want then? Are you still getting it? Do you still *want* it? Or is nostalgia holding you to a place that no longer meets your needs? You just might discover that you've switched your needs. What was important then just isn't important now. Or maybe the things you value have gotten perverted. You might have joined your corporation expecting a "Challenge," only to find that you're now spending your days waiting for retirement. Or that "Creativity" and "Power" have dwindled down to "Income" alone. Whatever your situation, it's vital to take a trip back in time to understand more about what you're getting *now*. The resentment or dissatisfaction you feel may simply be part of an old mind-set that is stunting your growth today . . . and could continue to do so in the future.

"WHERE DO YOU WANT TO BE NEXT?"

As Barbara Walters has said to many a celebrity, "What next?" Where do you want to be in one year? Five years? Ten years? Twenty years? Or, if it's easier to envision, where do you want to be by the time you're thirty, forty, and fifty? Once you spell out your future goals, whether it be on a legal pad or on a home computer screen, you can plan a present-day strategy to get them.

A young cost accountant named Sam decided that a raise bringing his salary up to $30,000 was appropriate for his position, age, and expertise. However, his request for a raise was turned down. "I *instantly* understood I had no future there," Sam told me. "I had been turned down without even a promise of when it would come through. The pyramid was just too steep to climb." Since Sam had planned a future strategy, he knew he'd better start looking around for a job that offered the money he wanted. Knowing his job search could take some time, he also went back to his boss and asked for more responsibility—not only to justify a raise in his present job, but to give him the experience he needed to meet his goals while he waited for the right opportunity to come along.

A careful analysis of these four questions will bring valuable insight to your ultimate decision. But let's leave your inner world for now and look at the corporate world around you, the external piece in your leave or stay equation. . . .

OUTER LIMITS

While your internal evaluation deals with your dreams and wishes, your external assessment is the bottom line in your decision to stay or go. It has to do with your corporation's health, and your role in its day-to-day routine.

How well is your company doing? Your department? Your industry as a whole? Maybe your department is doing badly and it's part of a corporation that's rapidly getting more and more depressed. A situation like this zaps energy and confidence unless you're involved in a team effort that's actively trying to correct the problems.

What about the management teams in your corporate world? Examine the people who are running the show. Look at the way they treat their employees, if they reward people for staying—or if they're just in it for themselves. Do you admire them? Are they competent? Do you trust them enough to guide the company through a bad spell?

Your own perceptive powers will go far in answering these questions, but to get an in-depth assessment of your corporation, investigate the annual reports and the trade journals. See what the press is saying about your company and the field as a whole.

The more you probe your corporate sphere, the faster you'll find results. You'll begin to see a pattern emerge; the reasons to stay may look bigger than the reasons to leave—or just the opposite.

Just when you thought it was safe to say, "I like my work, I like my company, and I want to stay," a career block can arise to throw your whole equation out of whack. Unlike the endless variety of variables you'll find in your personal internal and external fact search, there are four main kinds of blocks. Each one can kill a career, and each one has to be examined and understood before your leave or stay equation gets the grade.

CAREER BLOCKS

Remember the alphabet blocks you played with as a child? You'd pile one on top of the other until one false move sent the whole tower crashing to the ground. A career's balance is rarely that precarious, but there are four situations that are notoriously dangerous. Each one can build upon the other with deadly results.

Recognizing them can be the difference between a deft jump toward your goals—or a fumble with reverberating results.

1. Personality Clash

A personality clash between you and a colleague can make life miserable. A personality clash between you and your boss can be worse. You can always slam the door and walk away in your personal life, but a company expects you to work with difficult bosses and colleagues. They might be hard to take, but they are not necessarily a reason to leave. After all, you don't have to like each other to function as a team. Companies (and executive recruiters) will usually see it as a sign of professional maturity to rise above animosity. If you don't, they may very well consider it *your* problem. As a search professional with Management Recruiters explained, "Executive recruiters watch employment history. They will accept that a person has a disagreement or a personality conflict with one manager. More than that, it's a problem."

The consequences of this particular block hit harder the higher up the pyramid you are. If you're caught in a clash at the top, you'd better start your job search fast. If you don't get along with the president, your days are numbered. But if you're a middle manager, there's more room to maneuver. Listen to the words of executive recruiter Thorne Foster: "In top management, relationships are the name of the game. But if you're a middle manager having a personality conflict with the person above you, there are plenty of things you can do: find other managers to talk with; talk it out with personnel or your sponsor; or simply go around your boss. If a middle manager tells me he or she wants to leave because of a personality conflict, I have to wonder if it's a rationalization."

One bewildered woman had a real personality clash with a colleague. "He was very good at what he did, but he was a real toad. I didn't understand why I had to put up with him." She was above him in the corporate structure, but top management wouldn't let her fire him. In fact, management got so disgusted with her constant battles that *she* was forced out—not the man below her whom she disliked.

If you find yourself in the throes of a personality clash at your company, try to figure out why. And if it's in your best interest to ride it out, do so. Don't let a "toad" or a bad boss ruin your career.

2. *Corporate Culture Clash*

A conflict with one person is not always a reason to go, but a clash with a company's style and procedures is. Recruiters accept corporate culture clash as a fact of life. "We're in the business of minimizing risks," one recruiter told me. "We are not going to want to bring in people who will not get along in a corporate culture."

If you think you're being blocked by a corporate culture clash, you probably are. Like trying to put a round peg in a square hole, it's a difference you'll feel right away. Unfortunately, it's also a feeling we usually blame totally on ourselves. A company's unwritten culture—its ways of dressing and behaving, its values and the role models you're expected to emulate—is usually so strong that anyone who does not conform is considered wrong, a loser in the eyes of the majority rule.

It's a tough block to meet head-on. I've worked with countless intelligent, talented people whose careers were floundering because they liked to work in ways that were different from their culture. There are the careful, methodical problem solvers who are considered "slow and stodgy" in a seat-of-the-pants decision-making culture. Then there are the right-brained strategists cast adrift in a left-brain culture who will always be known as "weird." What makes this block so insidious is the fact that people tend to promote those who are just like themselves even if they really need someone with different skills for better balance.

If you're suffering from a corporate culture clash right now, don't try to be something you're not. In the long run you'll only find more misery. Cut your losses quickly—and find a more compatible home *fast*.

3. *Politics of Power*

Like corporate culture, every company has its politics. It's a fact of business life. As one recruiter told me, "People who complain about politics are often the people who don't understand the environment and can't adapt to it. They're considered suspect. The only time politics gets bad is when it gets in the way of work."

It's true that people do get fired for picking the losing side in a political war. But the outplacement specialists I spoke to told me more people get fired for *not* playing politics. Believing the old adage "Doing a job well is all you need to do," they'll get passed over when it comes time for promotions and raises. You have to let your talents be known. You have to play the game. This doesn't mean becoming a Roman emperor prototype, full of backstabbing intrigue, but it does mean developing a few advantageous liaisons. Colette Conroy, who has been an on-staff outplacement counselor with two Fortune 500 companies, says, "People who get fired often haven't made any political alliances. They think there's something wrong with it. They think it's slimy to even have an occasional lunch with the 'right' people who'll help them succeed."

Sometimes politics can affect you even when you're not an active participant on either side. If your boss is fired, you can get caught in the political aftermath. There's no question that this can be a tricky time, but don't fool yourself with the "With this new regime, things will stay the same" lie that binds. Examine your loyalties. Evaluate your strengths and make them known to your new boss. And continue to assess your leave or stay equation.

Similar political troubles brew when your mentor leaves. If you've been known as a one-person man or woman, you can be left wide open for a demotion, a loss of power, or, worse, the ubiquitous pink slip. This doesn't mean you shouldn't have a mentor. A study conducted among a thousand senior vice-presidents showed that 64 percent believed that part of their success came from a mentor relationship. So how do you avoid a "Catch-22" situation? Simple. Avoid becoming overly dependent on your mentor. Cultivate relationships with other Movers & Shakers as well. You'll be less vulnerable to the swings of political fate. Political blocks can turn into building blocks with the right strategy.

4. Performance Problems
This one is the killer block, the most crucial of the four. Performance deficiencies will stop you from reaching the top. Period. But the good news is that this is the one block that is most in your control. Analyzing and assessing your needs and your company's structure can turn your performance around from peaked to peak, regardless of whether you move on or not.

Believe it or not, everyone—even those who have gone clear to the top—has had to cope with deficiency problems. A study conducted by two behavioral scientists, Morgan McCall, Jr., and Michael Lombardo, showed that managers who have reached the highest levels had the *same* failings as those who got derailed along the way. They interviewed twenty-one top executives and twenty managers who'd almost reached the top but ultimately failed. All forty-one executives were astonishingly alike: 1) all were strong, but 2) each had one or more weaknesses that 3) caused career setbacks and serious problems that needed to be overcome. Here are the most common problem areas the researchers discovered:

   a. Insensitivity to others, using a bullying, intimidating manner
   b. A cool, aloof, and arrogant style
   c. Betrayal of trust, either by one-upmanship tactics or by not following through on a promise
   d. Overambition

e. Overmanagement of their people

f. Inefficient staffing of their departments

g. An inability to adapt to a boss with a different style

h. Too much dependency on a mentor

i. An inability to think strategically

j. Weak results showing downswing profits and lost accounts

Why did one group overcome their problems while the other did not? The derailed executives exhibited a host of unproductive responses. They got peevish. They tried to shout down the boss. Or they got defensive and became rigid. On the other hand, the executives who became CEOs showed a flexibility and a nondefensive attitude when faced with a setback. They used their energy to correct rather than deny their performance problem.

If you're confronting a performance block, there are ways to correct the situation. When you've made an error, ask yourself if you were unconsciously setting yourself up to be fired because you'd really like to be somewhere else. If not, take a lesson from the successful executives and be flexible. Chalk your problems up to being human. We all make mistakes. And one mistake—even a big one—will probably not destroy your career *if* you admit it and correct it. Paul Ray, Sr., an executive consultant, claims, "If you're any good, you're going to take risks—and that means you're going to have many successes and some failures. Meet your failures head-on. In most cases, the people you failed will appreciate your candor and you'll keep their support."

If your career has been hurt by one or more of these four problem areas, you're going to have to decide how serious the damage is—and if it can be repaired. The only way to assess career block aspects of your leave or stay equation is to listen to the feedback you're getting. Objective hearing is essential for a correct interpretation.

BREAKING THE WARNING SYSTEM CODE

When you get criticism from your boss, is it a warning that your career is in such trouble that you'd better look around? Or is it a bit of constructive advice? One way to get beyond your personal paranoia is to ask. I've found most people are remarkably honest if directly questioned in an appropriately businesslike manner. In fact, the personnel manager of a Fortune 100 company told me, "The most common problem is *not* that people weren't given the word about being in trouble. A boss has to give some kind of warning. The problem is getting people to *hear* it."

Signals can get crossed in more positive situations too. People who are doing extremely well don't always hear the good feedback because they doubt themselves.

To be sure you're "hearing correctly," assess your corporation's actions—which always speak louder than words. Are you getting good assignments? Do you have visibility? Are your promotions and raises comparable to those of your colleagues who have similar seniority? If so, you're doing fine.

But there's one hard-and-fast rule that's always a red-flag warning: *Beware of losing the goods*. When something is taken away from you, it's usually a sign you're in trouble—be it your large corner office, a perk, regular meetings with higher-ups, or a choice assignment.

Once the seriousness of your career block is determined, you have to ask yourself if it's likely to change. Is your problem a personality clash with your boss—or with the corporation as a whole? A female manager I interviewed was having a great deal of trouble winning a raise. After examining her situation, she realized that the company had an unwritten policy not to promote women. "The men were getting a piece of the action and I was getting taxi money home." She ultimately cut her losses and left for a better job with a less antiquated corporation.

However your career block situation stacks up, it's a vital part of your leave or stay equation. But don't start analyzing the data just yet. There's one more piece to look at before you can stamp your investigation closed.

THREE BLIND MICE

Unlike the "lies that bind" us to a job we hate, the following lies make you leave your job when you're not ready. These are the rationalizations that create job-hoppers, people who keep moving on and never establish the kind of commitment necessary for success. Even those with stable job histories can convince themselves to make a bad move instead of staying and working out their problems.

1. "I'm not happy, so I should leave."
Maybe. But no one is ever 100 percent happy in any corporate home. Every job has its problems. You have to decide whether the problems you're currently facing are ones that you'd find anywhere at this stage of your career . . . or if the unhappiness is part of the internal baggage you tote from place to place.

Is your job dull? What can be done to spice it up? Have you been transferred to the "minor leagues"? That *can* be a reason to leave if it's a demotion. But it just might be your company's strategy to teach you new skills. Is it a long-term transfer or a short-term move to prepare you for better things? *Ask.*

Of course, "I'm not happy" can be a very real lament instead of a whine. You could have had the goods taken away. You could be in the midst of a corporate culture clash. But check out your complaint before checking out of your home. "I'm not happy" can become a lifelong refrain.

2. "I'll get stuck if I stay."
Who says? Like the lover who leaves when the word *commitment* rears its ugly head, the job-hopper who sings this familiar song is destined to remain promiscuous and never establish healthy

104

roots. The crux is that you have to stay in a job long enough to accomplish something if you want to build a career. This is not to say that you shouldn't keep an eye out for more opportunities, but sometimes the best and the safest ones are found at home where you have a network and a basis of power. Most Fortune 500 CEOs are one-company men. And studies show that the majority of the balance have only moved once or twice.

While some job-hoppers switch out of a Peter Pan fear of growing up, there are those who move around to keep the adrenaline flowing. Still others are tuned into an internal time clock, changing companies the same way they once changed schools or grades.

Whatever the reason, no one intentionally wants to end up with an unstable job history. When does job-hopping begin to look bad? Each recruiter had a different definition. One told me, "Three jobs in five years begins to look like too many." Another believes people "shouldn't have more than three or four jobs by the time they're thirty-five or forty." But *all* recruiters stress that there are no hard-and-fast rules. What's more important is *why* a person leaves a job and *why* he or she accepts another offer.

How about you? Are you thinking of leaving because of a very real obstacle? Or are you just plain restless?

3. *"If I can't go up, it's out."*
Only one out of every twenty middle managers will make it to the top. Said one senior manager: "Almost everyone over forty has to face the fact they're going to be passed over." Cruel, cold words. But they're true. The pyramid narrows at its height. Furthermore, the average term for a CEO is only seven years. They're usually fired.

Despite these statistics, executive recruiters *expect* their clients to strive for the top job. As one said to me, "Someone who doesn't want to be president? What the hell is wrong with him? Never say that!"

Compulsive striving might strike you as strange. Why reach

for a goal that's not only almost impossible to attain, but so fleeting as well? Because it's difficult to decide you're not going up. And it's difficult to watch your friends doing better. We're simply expected to reach for the brass ring.

The question you have to ask yourself is if you really want to be at the top. If "Power" and "Prestige" are at the top of your Key Benefits card sort, go for it! Find the company you can lead. But make sure you have the skills needed for the job. You don't want to cut through one trap only to find another.

Research scientists are recently finding that there is a real "executive I.Q." that successful managers display. They are all adept at long-term thinking. They can comfortably juggle different information about different problems and rarely drop the ball. And they all adapt well to rapidly changing events.

One successful woman recently told me that she did not like managing people. Like many others who realize they lack this crucial ingredient to make it to the top, she switched to consulting work, where she can use her business analysis skills without the burden of managing a staff. If you want the "Power" but don't have the skills, you can also get ahead in one of the corporations that have "dual ladders."

Perhaps you resemble this brand manager: "At twenty-five, I sat around and laughed along with my colleagues about the lack of sixty-year-old marketing guys. But now I'm thirty-five, and it doesn't seem funny anymore." He had received his M.B.A. at Tuck, and he recently asked them for a printout of where all the marketing graduates are today. "I studied it, and I saw that those people who graduated ten or fifteen years ago and stayed with a Fortune 500 company weren't high up in the system. The ones who became presidents left their big corporations for smaller ones." He realized that if he wanted to make it to the top, he'd have to move. "But I figure the odds are against me. It's too much work. What I want now is a nice green pasture where I can spend a pleasant and self-respecting corporate life."

What about you? What does your Key Benefits List say? Are

you in danger of getting trapped by an ambition you really don't feel? Like Scrooge's ghosts, it can come back to haunt you and turn you into one of the three deadly has-beens:

THE WILD BORES
They're the ones with the big, florid faces. They drink too much and eat too much. They don't do much anymore but talk, dropping as many names as they can to pretend to be important. But no one is fooled.

THE THIN MEN
They're the other side of the has-been coin. Their faces are strained. Their lips are puckered from too many frowns. They don't like to talk at all—unless it's about saving money. They have a real sense of shame and self-reproach.

THE REBELS
They're filled with anger. Instead of using it constructively, they challenge the system by flaunting the dress code or by coming in late. They fight windmills while sabotaging no one but themselves.

To be forewarned is to be forearmed. *Don't* be a has-been. If you've always believed "It's up or out," but you've found yourself in a position a few rungs down, make peace with your life:

- *Accept* being passed over for promotion. What happened, happened. Use your energy to insure a positive future.
- *Commit* yourself to your work. Pretend you've just started your job—and make it better.
- *Find* something to excite you in your personal life. Think fun and challenge.

And above all, finish your leave or stay equation. Prevent the deadwood/has-been syndrome by making an active choice.

THE LAST-DITCH EFFORT

False pride should never push you away from a company you love. On the other hand, if "Power," "Challenge," and "Upward Mobility" really matter to you, you should definitely start a serious search for a better job. No one says you can't enjoy what you're doing in the meantime.

If you decide something is radically wrong after careful analysis, you do have to take action. But before flying the coop, try to make things right at home. Talk to your boss. Don't threaten. Don't show a desire to leave. Simply get that unbiased feedback. Talk about your goals and how, or if, the boss thinks you can reach them. Do your homework so your boss knows you're serious: make a list beforehand of all your responsibilities and contributions and the impact you've had on the corporation and your department. There's no place like home to get things back on the right track.

WHAT I THINK I AM

This is it. You've examined your internal feelings and needs. You've gathered the facts on your external corporate structure. You've faced your career blocks head-on and you've probed the "lies that bind" that could push you into a bad decision. Your leave or stay equation is complete and your choices should be clear:

1. Quit, but beware: it is usually more difficult and more stressful to find a job when you are unemployed.
2. Look around with every intention of leaving.
3. Look around just to check out other options.
4. Stay and change the problems you face.
5. Stay and put your decision on hold, hoping your storm cloud will blow over.

Whatever choice you make, you'll be able to decide more rationally than before. You'll be able to look at the whole picture and decide what's best for you and no one else. You're in the driver's seat.

If you feel that you must leave, you should do it with finesse. No bridges should be burned. In the next chapter you'll find the best ways to leave—and the best ways to say hello to your new corporate home. . . .

Chapter 8

A Good Exit and a Good Entrance

Good-bye . . .
"Just like in a love relationship, there's always the fear of how the other person will react when you tell them it's over."   —Young professional,
                                                                              Advertising agency

. . . and hello:
"I was expected to answer all these complex questions right off the bat—and I didn't even know the way to the men's room!"   —Senior manager,
                                                                              Electronics firm

"There may be fifty ways to leave your lover, but there are only two ways to leave a job: either you have another waiting, or you don't."

"I never said 'no' when a headhunter called. I was always open. You never know what's out there."

"After four years, I received a job offer I couldn't turn down. I left—but it was hard."

"When I left the 'womb' for my new job, I was terrified. But I was exhilarated too."

A Good Exit and a Good Entrance

Leaving a job is never easy. It's talked about over drinks, whispered about in the corridors of power, and hashed and rehashed when you toss and turn at night.

Some people need their back to the wall before they look for a new job. Some even sabotage themselves into getting fired. But there's an easier way: a civilized divorce.

We all understand how a marriage—even a bad one—provides benefits that are hard to leave. Both excitement and dread accompany the thought of leaving a mate behind. Divorce dramatically changes our circle of friends, our social life, and our daily pattern of living. Upset and loss alternate with feelings of hope and gain.

If any of this strikes a familiar chord, it should. By now you've begun to understand the deep emotional attachments that come part and parcel with your regular corporate check. You can pinpoint that sense of belonging, identity, and security you feel within your corporate family—and you've come to grips with it. You've discovered that you're not satisfied—and there's nothing you can do in your present home to change it. You're ready for divorce.

But it's hard to leave behind a comfortable life-style, a family and friends, and the benefits you are receiving (even if they are not the benefits you want). You hope to settle into a happy new relationship, but as with marital divorce, there's always the chance that the new "partner" will turn out to be another mistake —or worse, may be the beginning of a long series of unsatisfying liaisons.

Some of the things you've already learned from this book should soften much of the trauma involved in divorcing your corporation. But even after you've explored your leave or stay equation and you've decided with confidence that to leave is best, you still have to contend with the exit—and the equally important entrance to your new corporate home. Both can either wrench the wind from your sails—or can be handled with a minimum of emotional pain.

It's far more pleasant for you *and* your company if you can part on good terms. A well-planned, well-executed exit with the right job waiting lowers the stress of one of the most stress-producing situations in life. A civilized leave-taking allows you to take the good memories with you wherever you go.

So how is it done? As with the other corporate variables I've discussed, it takes some thorough research, some common sense, and an analysis of your position and the prospects you have at hand right now.

So much advice about finding a job is available that I will just top line a few ideas in this chapter. Basically, a good exit that leads to a good entrance involves these five crucial steps:

1. A firm decision to leave (or at least search)
2. Confidence in your abilities
3. Building bridges to the outside world
4. A successful job search
5. The final good-bye

Each step in a "civilized divorce" depends on the successful completion of the one preceding it. Leave-taking is always difficult, but as you examine each step one by one, you will find that by now you have completed a lot of the basic work:

Step 1:

A FIRM DECISION TO LEAVE (OR AT LEAST SEARCH)

Courage. You have to be certain before you embark on any new endeavor. Unless you've decided it's absolutely right for you to look or leave, you'll never be able to conduct a successful job campaign. You'll waiver back and forth and drain the energy you need to make a positive change.

Some people take years to make that final decision. The information in the previous chapter should help you speed up the process. The analyses you have performed should have heavily weighted either the pro or con side of your decision tree. You have discussed your situation with your immediate supervisor and you've checked out other opportunities within the company. You can now say with surety that it's right to look around.

Step 2:

CONFIDENCE IN YOUR ABILITIES

Once you've made that firm decision, you can start a serious job search. Before you polish that résumé or check out your first lead, you have to have the confidence to know what you want and to go out there and get it. It's a confidence that comes across in job interviews, the kind that lets part of you sell yourself while the other part sits back and thinks, "Do *I* want this job? Docs it utilize *my* skills and intelligence? Will it help *me* grow?" Knowing what you've got to offer is the key to an accurate appraisal of a prospective job.

How do you find that confidence and, even more crucial, keep it going during a search that's filled with no's and exhausting interaction?

Make lists. On an index card that you can carry around, write down your past successes, the things you've done that made you feel good, the accomplishments that made you proud. On the flip side of the card, note the compliments you've received on the job. Try to remember as many nice things that people have said as you can.

Before your next interview, take out your card and read it. It will provide a dose of positive energy that will go a long way in keeping your confidence level up.

Step 3:

BUILDING BRIDGES TO THE OUTSIDE WORLD

Finding a good new job has a lot to do with being in the right place at the right time. You can increase your odds if you build bridges to the outside world early instead of waiting until you need them. You never want to be caught in the position of this executive who had been passed over but couldn't leave: "I want to get out, but I feel paralyzed. I've lost my bridges to the outside world, and I have no idea how to build them back up."

This is a fact: 60 percent of all jobs are filled through networking. Professional contacts are the bridges to the outside that help you get that job. But it's important to "network" in other ways too. That means knowing the headhunters in your field and getting on their lists long before you need to. It means seeking out the people in your industry who can further your career. It means keeping your résumé up-to-date and impressive. It means keeping up with the trade journals and getting noticed.

At the top of the list are those executive search firms that have the jobs you want to know about. Let's cut through some of the mystique surrounding the almighty headhunters and see what they can—and can't—do for you.

First of all, a search firm is not an employment agency. While employment agencies will invite you to come in through ads in the paper, search firms never do. And they usually handle only jobs in the over-$30,000-a-year range. Search firms do have two things in common with employment agencies: 1) their clients are the companies who pay their fees—not you; and 2) they only keep a limited number of jobs on file at any one time.

"The probability of someone writing us and being considered for a job," says Bill Gould, an owner of a medium-size search firm, "is literally one in a thousand. We get forty thousand résumés a year and maybe forty are applicable to the jobs we're

114

working on at the time." Responding to a newspaper ad is also a long shot: a good ad in a major paper will pull up to two thousand résumés, but only two to five out of every hundred applicants get a phone call.

To increase the odds in your favor:

1. Avoid blanket mailings. Recruiters and employers spend an average of thirty seconds per résumé. The ones that don't a) shine and b) relate to one of the few positions available are either filed or thrown away. Use your time and energy to network instead.

2. Never turn down a headhunter's call—even if you're happy where you are. Like the Boy Scouts, always be prepared: always say you're happy with your job, but always be willing to hear about good opportunities. Headhunters like to think they're stealing you away from your firm. They know it's a game. You know it's a game. But it's one you have to play when you network. The headhunters will not usually give you the name of the firm where the position is open. They'll tell you the general locale, the salary, and the position. Recommend your friends for jobs you do not want. Act confident (recruiters can't see your index card over the phone) and tell them what might interest you. Above all, be aware of your role. Recruiters might be nice people, but they are not father confessors or friends. They will be "watching" you. File the headhunters name and phone number for the future.

3. When friends get good jobs, find out how. Get the name of the search firms and look over their résumés. Nothing succeeds like success, and if it worked for them, it just might work for you.

4. At first, think of job interviews as practice. You will be less nervous that way. Even if the position doesn't pan out, you will have improved your interviewing skills.

5. Keep your visibility up with articles that carry your by-line and letters to the editors about business affairs. Stay active in trade and civic organizations, and keep up with your former college deans. Make your promotion news by getting the details into print in the trade journals along with a good, recent photo.

It can mean the difference between getting lost in the shuffle and getting noticed by recruiters who scan these sources for candidates.

Here's an example of a chemist who turned his networking expertise into a better job. Blocked by a young boss who'd be staying for a while, he decided he'd better search for a position with more Upward Mobility. He began his networking at a yearly convention where he met a supplier he'd known in a former job. They started talking. "I had a bar set up in my room to be hospitable—and it worked." The supplier finally came around to mentioning another corporation that was looking for someone with a chemistry background. It was a good job, and the chemist was more than interested. He maneuvered the supplier into setting up a meeting with a representative from the company that had the open position. The chemist shook hands and began the standard line: "I'm happy where I am, but I'd be interested in talking . . ." A few months later the job was his.

What if you don't have the luxury of time to get your bridges solidly built? For crash courses:

- Make a list of everyone you know. Call them and tell them you're looking.
- Call the people *they* tell you to call. Ask if there are any positions open—or who else you might call.
- Use your contacts' names to open doors.
- Draw up an outstanding résumé and send it off. Even a long shot is worth pursuing when you don't have time.

Obviously, when you have to resort to the crash course, your boss is more likely to find out you are looking. Even with discreet long-term planning, there's no guarantee your job search will be confidential for long. References are always checked in one way or another. People talk. If you're about to be vested in some financial plan, you're better off waiting. As one senior manager said, "Any company might deny you benefits or a bonus if they find out you're looking before you're fully vested."

Each company has a different policy about job searching. For some, it's grounds for termination. For others, it's accepted as long as you've only responded to an interview call and have not been looking actively. Whatever your firm's views, if you're miserable, you should probably take the risk. "Most companies will not fire you if they like you," a personnel director at a consulting firm explained. "If they hear that you're looking, they'll try to keep you. In most places, problems only arise if your hold is tenuous, if you're having problems with your career."

How to best handle the risk factor? If your search is discovered, tell the powers that be that Company X came to *you* with a job possibility that was so attractive you had to explore it. Reaffirm your loyalty if you've decided to stay. Like telling a headhunter "I'm happy here, but . . . ," it's the steps to a tango you have to learn well.

Step 4:

A SUCCESSFUL JOB SEARCH

There's no doubt about it. Looking for a job is a full-time job. As one vice-president in charge of personnel put it: "Unless job hunters are making twenty-five to fifty contacts a week, they're not really looking." You're busy networking. Getting on the headhunters' lists. Listening. Talking. Attending conventions. Reading the trades, annual reports, and resource books.

Above all, you should be spending your time generating interviews. Without interviews, there can be no job offers. And without job offers, you're stuck where you are.

Interviewing for success is a trainable skill, but it does take time to understand its subtleties and techniques. Entire courses are devoted to the art of interviewing. Books have been written on the subject. Because information is so readily available elsewhere, I won't go into detail here, but I would like to pass along some advice.

A good interview has five stages. Understanding them can give you some control:

1. *Feeling each other out and breaking the ice.* Expect some small talk and then . . . be prepared with clear, concise answers to the difficult bottom-line questions in most employers' minds: What can you do for us? Why should we hire you? What are your goals? Why are you leaving your present job?

2. *Tentative probing about the job.* Ask the questions search experts do: How long has the position been open and why? How many people have held the position before? Why did they leave? The answers to these can go a long way in helping you analyze the situation—and prepare you for a good entrance. If there's been a high turnover, it can mean this is a trouble spot. If people have gone on to bigger and better things, you might too. Watch out for any long pauses. They can sometimes tell you more than words.

3. *Finding out what the employer wants.* Listen and observe. Is the employer really looking for what he says he wants? Maybe she can't really delegate authority. Maybe he won't spend the money for necessary changes.

4. *Keying your pitch to the employer's needs.* Make sure you know exactly what's going to be expected of you and for what you'll be responsible. (If you haven't received specific answers—beware!) Then discuss how you can meet the company's needs.

5. *Talking money—but never until interest is aroused.* You're in a better bargaining position if you can avoid talking money until they want you. When asked your current salary, use all your current compensation—salary, bonus, *and* benefits—when computing the figure.

But interviews alone do not a total picture make. Even if yours went well, there are still some things to look at before you say yes:

- *The Chief Executive Officer.* The values of the leader are pervasive and set the tone of the place. Is he the kind of person you respect?
- *The attitudes of the receptionists and secretaries.* It's a way of observing the culture firsthand. Are they off-putting? Too casual? Do they make you feel comfortable?
- *The corporate uniform.* Is it compatible with your tastes and standards? You don't want a corporate culture clash.
- *People who have recently been promoted.* Talk to them. Find out why they were promoted. Was it for good work? And who are the people held in esteem in the company?
- *Yourself.* Do you have the skills to handle the job? Do you admire the company's Movers & Shakers and its team players?

And last but not least, there's that something extra, the *je ne sais quoi* that makes you feel good about a potential new employer —or not. Is the chemistry mix right? As George Rossetter, president of a Dunhill branch says, "What kind of chemistry do you feel with your potential new supervisor? With your new peers? *Eighty percent* of any hire is chemistry. Even if you don't meet the exact qualifications."

The key to a successful job search is finding the job that's right for you. And the only way to ensure you're getting what you want is to ask questions—to the people in charge, to the people around you, and to yourself. Once you're hired you might not get the honest answers you need.

A Brief Pause:

ASSESSING THE ASSESSMENT

Congratulations! You've received that job offer. Now what? Once again it's time for an equation. List the advantages and disadvantages of both the new job and the old job in columns. Review your Key Benefits List. Are your needs going to be satisfied at this new job? Will it help you attain satisfaction in the future? Question your fear honestly. Is it merely nerves? Or an unsettling portent of things to come? As a recruiter told me, "I ask candidates if they have any doubts, because if they do, this job is probably not for them. Challenges can make you nervous, but deep-seated doubts are a whole other thing."

If your positives add up to more than your negatives, it's time for the last, but most reverberating, step. . . .

Step 5:

THE FINAL GOOD-BYE

A middle manager I know, whom I'll call Dan, worked at a consumer products company that had a hard-nosed policy about leaving. You had to pack up the day you gave notice if you were going over to the competition. When Dan received a better job offer at a competitor, he took it—but he wanted to enjoy two last weeks on the job to tie up loose ends and to have a going-away party. "I went to fairly lengthy means to make sure I wouldn't get kicked out. I even went to the company lawyer and agreed not to work on a similar consumer product for two years."

Not everyone will go to such lengths to get their two weeks. But the way in which you say good-bye can mean the difference between pain and bitterness or pleasant memories. It is so important a part of a civilized divorce that executive recruiters say inept handling of the process has actually derailed many a career.

It's crucial to pick the right time and place to tell your boss. Be prepared to feel nervous. You are leaving your home behind, and quitting is a painful rite of passage. But careful planning can help you avoid the pitfalls of a traumatic divorce:

1. *Never tell your friends first.* Make sure your boss hears it from you. He or she deserves that courtesy.

2. *Plan your resignation speech.* Tell your boss you liked your job and your company, but it was an offer you couldn't refuse. Remember your tango steps.

3. *Don't expect your boss to be happy.* As I've already discussed, even a Superboss will miss a right-hand man.

4. *Resist the urge to get things off your chest.* Stick it to them and they might stick it right back to you someday. You can never tell where or when the other person will turn up. One senior manager who conducted exit interviews described the "urge" this way: "Even when I asked *why* they were leaving, I didn't want to hear it. It always sounded like sour grapes, and I took it personally." Another manager told me that she doesn't tell anyone about the problems she saw: "Not to be selfish, but because I realized you can't do any good. If you leave them with bad feelings, they'll rewrite your history. If you stay in the industry, you'll have to have lunch with them sometimes. They might even hire me down the road. It's just too small a world to risk retaliation."

5. *Beware the counteroffer.* It goes something like this: "We have plans for you that have been scheduled to start in two months. Guess I should have told you." Or "There's reorganization afoot that will mean a significant promotion for you in the near future." Or "We'll match your new offer." Or "The president would like to meet us for lunch before you make your final decision." It sounds flattering, right? Wrong. In many companies your loyalty will always be questioned. You made a decision to leave because the situation wasn't good for you. They're offering the counteroffer because you threatened to leave. Most companies call that blackmail. Listen to the words of a top executive recruiter: "Maybe you can do it once. Never more. And it's real dangerous . . . I always ask why a position needs to be filled and I'm often told 'the person in the job now tried to quit last year.'"

There are times when it is right to accept a counteroffer: when you really like the company and they really want you. However, understand that many counteroffers are made only to keep you until you can be replaced.

6. *Expect to feel some pain*. But don't let it hinder you. After all your careful analysis, you know what you're doing is right. Good-bye is as much a part of life as . . . hello.

The Honeymoon

Now that you've said good-bye to your old job, what's the best way to say hello to the new one? A good entrance is just as important as a good exit. Though much advice on how to get a good new job is available, there is very little about making sure that new job fulfills its promise. That first month and that first year can either make you or break you. Certain tasks must be accomplished quickly. Others must wait. Where do you fit in?

As you sit behind your new desk in your new office, staring out at your new view, you're probably wondering why you ever moved. The feeling you have might be compared to a roller-coaster ride. Here you are, fresh from having pulled off a brilliant coup—and you're terrified. Don't worry. It's natural. The anxiety you feel will dissipate in time.

In the interim, concentrate on showing a good face to your brave new world. First impressions are important: be energetic, be enthusiastic, and be willing to listen. Be wary of spouting such pearls of wisdom as "This is the way *we* did it back at. . . ." No one on your new team wants to hear it.

Stifle the urge to act quickly. While your perspective is fresh, do as one senior manager does: "I spend the first sixty days making at least a hundred and fifty notes to myself—from 'I don't like the toilet paper' to 'This guy has got to go.' " Remember, you're not expected to know everything right away. It's okay to admit you just don't know . . . yet.

It helps to be organized. Before instituting any major changes, make a short-term plan that will get you going on the right track. Though it varies from task to task and level to level, your goals should always include:

1. Getting the boss to believe you're the right choice.
2. Establishing good relationships with your supervisor, your management team, and your underlings—encouraging ideas and opinions.
3. Beginning a tentative judgment about the capabilities, strengths, and weaknesses of your management team and the company as a whole.

Once you've achieved all three, you'll have the confidence and the backing you need to act.

When it comes to action, timing is once again the key. Listen to executive recruiter Peter Grimm: "It's important to remember what level you've come in at and what you've been brought in for, whether you're expected to clean house in a company with a lot of problems or if you're starting in a good one. If you're a big wheel, you can take your losses right away. Two years down the road, cleaning house won't be looked at as favorably."

You have to know your role. At one level, certain behavior can look like a great threat. At a higher one, you'll be a savior. One man who runs a major publishing house was fired from his first marketing job in publishing because he kept telling everyone that they were doing everything wrong. He was considered insufferably brash then. He is considered a marketing genius today.

When you come in at a higher level, you will not only want to make changes, they'll probably be expected. But how do you get the feedback you need to make the right changes at the right time? You can't always ask questions, because subordinates will often tell you what they think you want to hear. You'll have to trust your observational skills more. Watch your CEO; actions will speak louder than words:

123

- What does he want you to accomplish—and when?
- What does she think of the vital few people around her?
- What decisions does he want to make for himself?
- What reports and feedback are you supposed to give?
- How often does she want to see you?
- Should you drop in or write memos?

One senior vice-president I interviewed shared his successfu system for making a good entrance: "I show my energy, m, strength, and my high expectations right away. I can get soft late . . . I always talk to consumers before my own people, and always talk to my sales force before talking to executives. Within the first two weeks I talk to everyone in my department—from the secretaries on up. I make a six-month and a twelve-month plan for myself, and I revise them every ninety days. I ask all my people to submit their goals to me in writing. If the people are good, I want to help them grow. If they want to leave, I'll help them find another job."

As this manager's system proves, a good entrance, like a good exit, is the result of careful planning and understanding—mixed with common sense and the guts to take the plunge. A new corporate marriage can create a whole new life—with all its inherent excitement, challenge, and wonder. "I want" can become a positive "I do."

But what if you don't want to change jobs within the same field? What if you what to divorce not only your corporation but your entire career?

Chapter 9

Divorcing a Career

"I have the feeling that somewhere in the universe there's
something I do exquisitely, but I haven't found it yet."
—Writer,
Public relations firm

I haven't been a psychologist forever. As an undergraduate I
majored in business administration, and I made my living
as an economist when I was first starting out. But something
nagged at me. The work just wasn't giving me enough satisfaction. After much soul-searching, similar to the self-analysis I've
already outlined, I decided to make the switch from business to
psychology. Not being one to do things halfway, I applied to
Columbia University's Ph.D. program. My friends thought I was
crazy—especially the ones who knew something about the field.
I had no training, no background—how could I possibly get into
one of the best and most difficult programs in the country?

Though it did take a lot of blind courage, I didn't leave everything to chance and a confident air. I spent one solid year prepar-
ing myself: reading every book I could find on psychology,
studying for the Graduate Record Examination, building up
twice as many recommendations as I needed, and approaching
the application with a marketing strategy designed to show how
my skills as an economist could be utilized as a psychologist. I
was accepted.

125

Unfortunately, a few friends reacted more with anger and jealousy than joy. They had wanted to go back to school or make career changes, but had failed to pull it off. Why was I accepted while these better qualified and equally talented friends weren't? Simply because I applied—*and they didn't*. I threw everything I had into getting accepted. If I had been rejected, I would have continued to reapply until I got a yes—despite the odds against me.

I successfully changed careers midstream and so can you. But it does take tenacity and a lot of work. Moving to another job is difficult enough, but moving to an entirely new field is even tougher. However, for many people, it's the only way to find true satisfaction in their working lives. Sometimes when a marriage breaks apart, the seeds for a whole new life you couldn't even have imagined are planted. Similarly, divorcing a career can open up a host of new possibilities and happiness. It can be done. And this chapter will begin to show you how.

SOMETHING'S HAPPENED

The lucky ones know what they want—and work for it. The less fortunate just know that something's wrong. Do you feel impatient every time you sit down at your desk? A nagging doubt? Or a growing excitement about all those other possibilities out there —if you just knew how to reach for them?

When you discover your career is not right, there's no thunderbolt. As one middle manager said: "I wasn't smitten like Paul on the road to Damascus. The decision to move builds gradually; it's like a toothache that keeps aching until you can no longer ignore it."

It's hard to admit you're on the wrong track, especially after having invested money in an education or time in a career. It's unsettling to realize that you've been fulfilling others' expectations instead of your own.

126

But there comes a point when you simply can't hide your head in the sand anymore. Something's got to give. For some people, it's their health. They'll begin to drink too much or get ulcers. The personal life of others is affected. They'll start an extramarital affair or take out their anger on their family. Still others will fail on the job so the company will be forced to fire them.

It doesn't have to be this way. You can do something constructive before you hit rock bottom. Life is too brief to waste it in a job you hate. If you've explored all the avenues open to you within your chosen field and you're still not happy, you might need a different career.

THE TIME CLOCK

It's easier to think about changing careers in our twenties. We've just entered the adult world. We're just beginning to define our interests and values, transforming those interests into an occupation. We are so young and inexperienced that it's very natural to make mistakes.

My husband was twenty-six when he left engineering for a career in advertising. It was difficult to turn his back on his Mobil Oil job and his double degree in chemistry and chemical engineering. But it would have been much harder if he'd waited.

The real crisis comes as one becomes more and more entrenched in a job, in a mortgage, and other responsibilities. The pressure reaches its peak as the decade years arise—the Big Three-0, Four-0, and Five-0—when it's natural to reevaluate our lives. Each new decade signals that time is slipping away—and stirs the need to become one's own person. We begin to feel an urgency to be what we still can be with the time we have left.

Mid-life crises are very real. It is during such crises that most people think about changing careers—and actually do something about it.

It happens all the time. People who've spent their lives making

127

money and becoming successful suddenly get the itch to nurture kids or do something for society. On the flip side of the coin are the teachers, social workers, and mothers who get the desire to enter the corporate world and make more money.

This flip-flopping is illustrated by a letter I received from a friend, a social worker in her forties, who'd become dissatisfied with her career: "I'll be looking for work in a field other than social work. One that I hope will pay better and give me less responsibility for other people's lives. You will, of course, recognize mid-life crisis when you see it!"

THE CAREER SWITCH ITCH

In addition to the natural process of aging, there are other situations that motivate us to move on to another career:

1. *When tragedy strikes your family,* there's a tendency to re-evaluate what's important to your life. As one successful career woman said to me, "My whole perspective on life has changed as a result of my child's accident. I had no idea that something could happen to me, my kids, or my husband. I never thought about tomorrow before. If I can make my family happy, that's enough for me right now."

2. *The birth of a child* creates a natural transition for many women. I started Columbia two weeks after my son was born. When I gave birth to my daughter, I left the clinic where I worked to start my private practice.

3. *When the children grow up and leave home,* many husbands and wives change their life-styles. Homemakers often go to work full-time, while businessmen may cut back their hours or switch fields.

4. *Being passed over or fired from a job* is a time when transformations take place. For many, it's seen as an opportunity to explore new horizons rather than a dead-end stop in the Twilight Zone.

5. *Great success* can cause a reevaluation as well. One such successful forty-year-old man told me, "I've already had my own business for years now and I'm doing really well. I've achieved my goals and I've made enough to retire. There's no longer any challenge. The trouble is I could go in ninety different directions. Should I go into another business? Should I start consulting? I think what I'd really like to do is study history for two years and teach."

6. *Retirement* gives people a chance to change. The man who produced Scrabble did so after he retired—turning a hobby into an extremely profitable venture. The owner of Cuisinart, Inc., started from scratch—with the extra time he had after retiring. Recently, the president of Bloomingdale's in New York took his retirement early, because "when you get to age fifty you wonder if it isn't time to make a move into something new." And a successful corporate administrator I interviewed also retired early to run a Catholic community and family service.

It's never too late to change careers. But it can take time, as it did for that new Catholic Charities director, who spent five years doing volunteer work on weekends in order to explore different options. On the other hand, the switch can be quick in coming. A case in point is the businesswoman in her forties who came to me for counseling. When her vocational interest test showed me she might be happier in the ministry, she applied to divinity school, sold her house, and prepared to move to Denver to go to school—all within three weeks! In a recent letter she writes: "I may be a little atypical, but not that far afield from a lot of women because I'm doing in my early 40's what I should have done in my 20's. I'm so peaceful now that it's hard to recall the stresses."

And there will be stress. We already know the stress involved in making a change, but it's magnified tenfold when you are not just leaving behind a corporate family, but a whole way of life. There's the added stress that many people simply won't understand what you're doing. In fact, they might feel so threatened, they'll fight it all the way. As one man who recently went through

129

a career switch ruefully said: "It's a time when you find out who your real friends are." Then there's always the stress-producing fear that you won't be able to cut it in a different field. You might look foolish or, worse, you might have to go back to your old corporate home, hat in hand, and ask them to forgive and forget —and take you back.

But the stress is worth it if it's really time to change careers. And the key word is *accept:*

- *Accept* that you're going to have stress. But keep your mind on your goal instead of that stress.
- *Accept* that many people will not understand what you're doing. It's upsetting, but remember that wanting to please other people may well be what put you on the wrong track to begin with.
- *Accept* that life is a series of chapters where nothing is lost. Something valuable is learned from all your corporate homes. Each career move, good *or* bad, is but one of those chapters en route to self-discovery.

But the biggest change you'll have to accept is less money—at least in the beginning.

MONEY MATTERS

There may be no way of getting around it. Chances are you'll have to take a pay cut to change fields. When you're married with children, a pay cut can hurt badly. If change is necessary and a loss of income unavoidable, discuss the money issue openly with your family. Work out a budget. Get their support and then start tightening your belt.

Unfortunately, money can be the issue that stops you cold— especially if it is one of your Key Benefits. As one woman told me, "I'm just not prepared to go back to school or begin earning

$12,000." She worked her way around the problem by staying where she was but finding more satisfaction in her personal life.

Location has a lot to do with the money factor as well. A senior manager living in Westchester County simply couldn't take a pay cut to change his career. "Not having a big income would mean I couldn't keep up with my friends—and I care about that very, very much." Instead of staying in a career he finds unfulfilling to maintain his life-style, he's considering a move to North Carolina —where the living is cheaper.

Moving can be an answer for some. As Florida employment agency owner Virginia Vinson says, "Some of the happiest people I've seen are those who go from white-collar to blue-collar jobs. They love being without a suit and being casual. They love the different pace. But this is in St. Petersburg, where people on the whole are less status conscious."

Don't start checking out the real estate market in Florida just yet. There are several ways to cut the risk—and your monetary loss—without moving to a different state.

If you're earning a good salary, why not try out your second career as a part-time endeavor first? Not only will you discover if it's really the spot for you, but you can continue to earn money in your present job. Do volunteer work in your spare time like the corporate administrator who became the head of the Catholic Charities agency.

If you need to go back to school to pick up the required credentials, why not take advantage of night school, where you can get the credits without giving up your daytime job? One corporate manager I know went to law school at night for several years. When she passed the bar, she divorced her career, but not her corporate family: she arranged a move from finance to the legal department.

WHAT I WANT TO DO . . . I THINK

It's wonderful to think about all the exciting possibilities out there just waiting for you to grab them. But what if you're wrong? What if that second career you've always dreamed of is more an *avocation* than a *vocation*? None of us wants to end up like the financial analyst I know who pulled up stakes and lived to regret it. Two years after trading in his pinstripes for overalls and a farm in upstate New York, he realized that he hated farming even more than Wall Street.

To avoid such a disastrous mistake, you can go to a career counselor to discover what you want to be with vocational tests. If you don't have the time or the money, you might want to try the following exercises I use in my private practice to help my clients switch careers with confidence:

1. Daydream. Turn your fantasies into productive planning. Think of every job you ever wanted to have. Write them down. Mentally try each one on for size to see how it feels.

2. Use your public library. Take out *The Dictionary of Occupational Titles* and *The Occupational Outlook Handbook*. Run your finger down the index, making note of any occupation that strikes your fancy. Don't be realistic right now. Don't limit yourself. You're an explorer searching new worlds. Don't think about anyone else but yourself—what *you* think sounds fun. You can get more realistic about what may or may not be practical later on. For now, what you need are ideas and direction. Analyze your list to see if your interests are clustered in a particular field —or if any occupation brings a "Eureka! That's it!"

3. Test your interest. One of my clients, a commercial artist, had always dreamed of being a doctor, and she continually berated herself for not having the discipline to go to medical school. When I gave her a vocational interest test, she scored far more like an artist than a doctor. Realizing she had made a good choice, not a lazy one, she could put her daydreams aside and concentrate on her art—without uprooting her life. Another way

132

to see if what you dream is what you want comes via a college catalogue. If you've always dreamed about becoming a doctor, take a pre-med course. If you want to know more about computers, there's a course tailor-made for your specialty. Schools and universities offer countless courses on almost any subject you can think of. Check them out. See if your dream is grounded in reality.

4. *Volunteer.* Becoming a volunteer gives you a chance to try a job on a much higher level than if you came in as staff. A television producer I met began her career switch from motherhood to TV by volunteering at the local educational station.

5. *Become an expert.* Read everything you can on the subject that interests you. Learn the jargon and the buzz words that are used in the field.

6. *Network.* Talk to everyone in the field. Make appointments and ask questions. Tell them you're researching the industry for a career switch. If you want to keep your plan quiet, tell them you're writing an article or gathering information for a course. The contacts you'll make can help if you decide the field is the right one for you.

PRESS FOR SUCCESS

You've done your soul-searching. You've tested the waters. You can say with confidence that almost everything about your chosen field feels right. You're ready to take the plunge. The time has come to make the switch.

A successful switch takes careful planning:

- How much work are you willing to put into the switch?
- How much will you give up in terms of money and prestige?
- How can you sell yourself?
- How can you make your crazy idea work?

133

Answering these questions is a lonely job. Planning a career change is, unfortunately, a one-man proposition. As one executive recruiter told me, "This is the time when employment agencies and search firms are the least helpful. We can help people advance up their career ladder. We can help people do what they're doing now in a new industry. But we can't help people who want a complete career switch, because corporations don't retain us to search for people who want to do something different."

The exercises I've outlined can help you plan out a strategy. Vocational counselors can lend support. And a little Yankee ingenuity can go a long way toward a successful change. Think "If I can't sell my experience, I'll sell my motivation" instead of "I can't do that. It's impossible."

Here are two people who made the "impossible" come true:

Tom went from administrative work at a large, bureaucratic corporation to marketing vice-president of a cable television system. "I decided I would end up being crushed by the bureaucracy," he told me. "I wanted to go into something more fun. I began to identify my goals. I assessed my skills to see how I could use them in my new field. I did a lot of networking and basic research until finally—at last!—I got an interview with this cable company. During the interview, the president said to me, 'Your background is interesting, but, Tom, you don't have any cable experience.' I didn't let it throw me. I replied, 'But let me show you how I've been successful with new things in the past. Let me show you how I've been handling my career switch—how I've defined my goals, my plans, how I'm approaching you. Don't you think I can use the skills I'm using now?'" Tom got the job.

Brenda is another success story. She made the "impossible" career switch from psychologist to director of human resources of a medium-size utility company, earning $50,000 a year plus an additional $20,000 in tax-free perks. "I went to the library every day after work for two solid years, researching the personnel field," she explained to me. "Then I drew up a map with a radius of how far I'd be willing to commute, using Standard and Poor's *Standard Corporation Descriptions* and Dun and Brad-street's *Million Dollar Directory* to see which corporations had offices within my radius. I also used these books to see what the corporations near me did and how they rated, further narrowing my list. Then I sat down and wrote two hundred and fifty letters to the presidents of the corporations that interested me. I even checked them out in *Who's Who* to see if there was some way to make the letters personal. I only got twelve interviews, but I kept telling myself, I only need *one* job. I read annual reports. I read business books and learned the jargon. And during those twelve interviews, I showed how my skills as a psychologist could be used effectively in business." Brenda ended up not with one but with three good job offers. She actually had to decide which job to take.

Lonely, yes. But intelligent career-switch planning can guarantee you won't be alone for long.

THE ENTREPRENEUR

What if your daydreams are less about changing careers and more about being your own boss? Starting your own business can be a reality too. There are countless ideas that could make you money—from inventing the ultimate rat trap to opening a home video store. As the founder of Atari said, "The critical ingredient is getting off your butt and doing something. It's as simple as that. A lot of people have ideas, but there are few who decide to do something about them now. Not tomorrow. Not next week. But today. The true entrepreneur is a doer, not a dreamer."

A McKinsey study of one hundred entrepreneurs who founded "mid-size" companies (generating $25 million to $1 billion in sales) prove Atari's founder right. All one hundred showed "a rare ability to innovate in the face of adversity, a bootstrap men-

135

tality, and a perseverance to the point of obsession. They find a way to get the job done, no matter what."

Just like successful career switchers, successful entrepreneurs do not get overwhelmed by the impossibility of the task. They make the impossible come true by thoroughly researching the business they want to get into, living the business once they are in it, working incredibly hard, and devoting years to achieve the results they want.

Unfortunately, eight out of ten new businesses fail within the first three years because they haven't been thought through. Careful planning is just as crucial to the successful entrepreneur as it is to a publicity director who wants to become a stockbroker. You can't simply translate a love of food into your own restaurant. Before you even raise the money you'll need, you have to know the clientele you want to reach, the markup, and the menu. You have to know what to buy, where to buy it, and how much you'll need from the very first moment you think ambience, good food, and white linen tablecloths. Behind every successful new venture you'll find a solid business plan and adequate financing to carry it through the early lean years.

Let's say you've done your research. You've taken some courses and you've honed your business skills. You're ready to open shop, but should you be thinking small—or should you start big? It all depends on what's most comfortable for you. One brand manager who left a large consumer products company to open up her own market research firm started small and worked her way up. "I told my friends I was available to run market research groups. One of them got me hired for a job. This established my experience. Then I picked up a second piece of business and went from there."

On the other end of the continuum is a woman who is planning to start a manufacturing company in a big way: "I decided I would need a couple of million dollars right off the bat. If I'm going to do anything, I'm going to do it right—with good package design on up. I've already started talking to some venture capital firms. I'm not one to start a business in my basement."

Whether small or big, entrepreneur or career-switch candidate, there's one thing all these people have in common: a dream that's turned into reality with careful planning, self-confidence, and tenacity.

They also show a willingness to compromise. One man I interviewed wanted to leave his public relations job at a bank to become an advertising copywriter. The only positions he could get were trainee spots. He didn't want to be an "elder" trainee, and companies were reluctant to hire a thirty-five-year-old for "a twenty-two-year-old's job." Instead he became a writer for a public relations firm, using his skills in a different way in a very different atmosphere from his boss.

Take your cue from this manager who wanted to switch careers: "When I thought about my career change, it was always a move *to* something I wanted rather than away from something I disliked. Of course I got discouraged, but I didn't stop looking until I succeeded." It's this kind of thinking that will make *you* succeed. It can happen. All the people I've written about in this chapter are happily working in a new career. If they can do it, so can you.

You've got to live your own life, and if that means divorcing a corporation or a career, it has to be. But what if you're not the one "filing the suit"? What if the other party asks for the divorce and the choice is not yours to make?

Chapter 10

Unrequited Love: Getting Fired

"I never thought it would happen to me."

—Middle manager,
Fortune 100 company

Burned. Got the ax. Let go.

There's nothing like the harsh-slap-in-the-face, floor-opening-up feeling of getting fired. It can be as devastating as hearing your wife say, "I've had it. Good-bye." Or watching your husband finger his tie while he says, "I've met somebody else."

The company has divorced you, pure and simple—and divorce is always hardest on the person who is left.

Let's face it: you are a victim. But you don't have to remain one. Just as in a real divorce, the months afterward can lead to tremendous growth, a rebirth that takes you down a road of new opportunities you never thought possible. A vice-president of a large paper company told me about an M.B.A. who hadn't been working out: "He was a smart and personable kid, but he was lazy. He got in late and he left early. He was told to shape up, but he didn't. He figured the company would never fire him, but they did. He then went out and found a new job—and received three promotions in three years."

A friend of mine had no such problem with performance, but she got fired just the same. A political upheaval cost her the job she'd had for fifteen years. After several months the shock finally wore off, and she cautiously started her own business. Two years later, she is happier—and richer—than ever before.

It has happened to the best of us, at one time or another, in the happiest of corporate homes. But as these two examples prove, "unrequited love" *can* mean never having to say you're sorry. . . .

A DEATH IN THE FAMILY

Divorce is never easy. If you've just been fired, the last thing you can imagine is ever feeling happy again. Right now the only bright spot is that ice clinking in your martini glass. A marketing director I know described herself as acting like "a spurned lover spying on my man." She'd walk past her former office building, looking longingly up at the windows, before she got back on her feet.

This is not unusual, especially when a company has fostered a family feeling, holding itself out as a secure nest in a cold, cruel world. As an ousted member of a New Maternalistic company, you're going to feel a tremendous sense of disillusionment when you discover the corporate family was a sham.

When the firing seems to come out of left field, the adjustments are even harder. "It's like they pulled off my arms," said a recent managerial victim, "and now I'm trying to put them back on."

I've seen enough people in similar situations to know there really is a light at the end of that bleak tunnel. It's all a question of understanding the process of being fired—and planning a positive recovery strategy. It can be done!

FIRING UP

You are not alone. Studies show that up to 35 percent of us are fired at one time or another in our lives. And every time it happens, the victim feels the same way you do now: terrible. And very, very scared.

That sinking feeling is a vital part of the healing process, a necessary step to getting over being fired and getting on with your life.

Psychiatrist Elisabeth Kübler-Ross discovered that there are six stages of emotion that people go through when they learn they have a terminal illness. Marriage counselors realized adults faced with divorce go through the same process. Career counselors see these stages* with people who have been fired:

1. Denial
2. Anger
3. Bargaining
4. Depression
5. Acceptance
6. Hope

The trouble really begins when people get stuck in one of the negative stages. They stay at the same plateau, never reaching the final step . . . hope. Let's go over each stage one by one so you can avoid getting emotionally trapped.

---

* Not everyone goes through all six stages nor does every person always follow this particular order.

Stage 1: DENIAL

"THEY REALLY MEANT THE JOHN SMITH IN ACCOUNTING."

None of us likes to accentuate the negative. It's much more comforting to pretend all is well rather than recognize a threat.

Take the case of Bill, a twenty-seven-year-old junior member of a small mortgage banking company in California. "The owner had a lot of charisma," Bill told me during one of our sessions. "We'd always be reading newspaper articles about him going to important places and parties. Then one Monday, the lead article in the paper reported how he was caught giving and taking bribes . . ."

Bill and the rest of his coworkers decided to ignore the headlines. Everyone pretended it wasn't true. "Our boss wouldn't steal. And even if he did, it was a problem with the man. The company was still sound."

By the second week, it was getting harder to live that lie. The two youngest members of the firm were fired. And during the third week, only Bill and one other man were left. "It felt like a meteor had crashed through my life, but I refused to admit how much trouble the firm was in. I kept so busy trying to figure out what the company should do that I avoided thinking about myself." He managed to hang on for three months before the company completely folded.

Bill refused to leave the now defunct office. He began renting the space himself. "I kept thinking some great deal would come walking through the door."

His denial lasted over six months—until he had no money left to pay the office rent. It took the harsh reality of being broke to force Bill to get a job and rebuild his life. But once he started, he didn't stop. Now, ten years later, he owns a very successful mortgage banking firm—and he never looks the other way when trouble brews.

Bill isn't the only one who's ever gotten stuck in the denial stage. I've interviewed many other competent professional people who kept up a charade. Some don't even tell their spouses they were fired. They get dressed, leave the house, and walk the streets until 5:00 P.M. each day, magically hoping their fate will change. Often, like Bill, it takes a financial crisis—or the energy derived from anger—to take control of their lives.

Stage 2: ANGER

"I HAVE A BLACK BELT IN KARATE AND YOU'LL BE SORRY."

Once you've passed the denial stage, anger may set in. It can be debilitating if you let it eat at you for too long a time—or it can be used to spur you on.

John's anger made him rigid, holding onto dreams and avoiding an effective job search. He'd been an owner/manager of a suburban Long Island restaurant, investing all his savings and thousands of hours to build it into a profitable venture. But John needed money. When a restaurant chain offered to buy the place, letting him stay on as manager, he said yes and signed the deal. A year later, the chain fired him. John was given no notice.

Needless to say, John was furious. "They put one over on me." His anger and hurt were beyond anything he'd ever felt before. He couldn't stop brooding over what happened to him, picking it apart and obsessively talking about it. Job interviews went poorly; the huge chip on his shoulder branded him a prospective troublemaker.

John stayed at this level for several months, lashing out at everyone, especially his family. Finally he enrolled in a three-month business administration course sponsored by a major university. This positive step enabled him to go on. He discovered, much to his surprise, that he didn't even like the restaurant busi-

142

ness. For the first time in years, he is giving himself time to explore other business opportunities, to enjoy his family and a long-dormant passion for music. A no longer angry John told me, "In many ways I'm in better shape than I ever was before."

Other people use anger to keep them going during the depressing aspects of a job search. A woman, whose job was eliminated at ITT, described a daydream she continued to have: "I would get this wonderful new job and then I would stand in front of the ITT building with a bullhorn. I would call the chairman, the president, and my boss to the window. When they looked down at me, I called them every rotten name in the book. I made them admit they were fools for firing me." When she found a good new job, the daydreams stopped. Her anger and need for revenge were in the past.

Stage 3: BARGAINING
"I'LL EVEN THROW IN THE KIDS."

Once we've passed through denial and anger, we have to face the bargaining stage. It doesn't always mean knees-to-the-floor begging, but bargaining is a plea. And at this stage, it often lacks the self-respect that backs up effective bargaining. Desperation shows. If a company—any company—will please, please hire us, we'll pledge to work harder—*and* cheaper. Or we'll appeal to a "higher authority," promising to tithe for the next ten years if God will change our fate.

Pam found the courage to bargain effectively when she was fired from the chemical company where she'd worked as a computer programmer for five years. At first her job had been terrific, but when she was transferred to a new division, she had a personality conflict with her new boss. Nothing improved their steadily worsening relationship. She should have left, but she didn't. When the final pink slip came down, Pam wanted to slink out of there as fast as she could. "I wanted to die." But a friend of hers convinced her to go in and talk to her boss. Pam figured she had nothing to lose. She pleaded with him at first, telling him how hard she'd always worked, how she'd always done the assignments he'd asked for on time, how she'd been with the company so long it felt like family. She said she'd do anything to stay on.

The bargaining didn't help her keep the job, but she did get a compromise: Pam was able to stay on the payroll until she found a new job. She got one in three months—without begging.

Stage 4: DEPRESSION

"LIFE IS MISERABLE AND SO AM I."

This is the stage most of us get stuck in, because looking for a job *is* depressing. It's a series of no's (and blows) until we receive that one good yes. Unfortunately, it's also the most insidious. Depression saps the energy and motivation we need to organize an effective job search. Our self-image falls to zero. Our confidence is nonexistent. What makes it worse, we project that picture to a prospective employer. Sitting on the other side of the desk, we're silently saying, "I'm nothing. I need the money, so if you want to throw me a bone, I'll take it. But I'll probably screw up." It's not exactly the mark of confidence your interviewer is looking for.

Depression is also the time of mourning. Everyone has his or her own time schedule when it comes to grief. For Janice, a single, forty-eight-year-old woman, the loss of her job triggered the deepest depression of her life. "I suffered greater grief when I was fired than when my mother died. I lost my identity and my belief in my abilities. I was stupid, a loser. I kept looking in the mirror, noticing my gray hair and wrinkles and wondering who would hire me." Janice felt all her strength drain away, even though she'd been fired because of budget cuts and through no fault of her own.

But it didn't matter to Janice. She was miserable and very

frightened. She was haunted by the fear that she would never get another job, that she would become a bag lady. Yet she kept up a façade and plunged into a job search, and two months later she found another home. But she has permanent scars. "I always have an updated résumé. I don't speak up very often in my new job, even though I used to be open and assertive."

Still, Janice is one of the lucky ones. Some people get so stuck in a depression that the whole situation becomes too painful to bear. Without their corporate family and their professional success, life becomes meaningless. Liz Peer, a well-known senior editor at *Newsweek,* committed suicide when she lost her job. Though she's an extreme example, unfortunately there are many who let depression sap their energy, keeping them permanently unemployed.

Depression can be binding, but for most of us, it leads to the final and best stages: acceptance and hope.

Stage 5: ACCEPTANCE

"WHAT IS . . . IS."

Depression is dismal. The whole world looks black. But with time, grief falls away. With the right kind of professional help or simply good, solid support from family and friends, we begin to stop beating ourselves. We begin to accept our situation. We begin to understand it's not the end of our life, but the loss of one job.

Like life itself, acceptance is a paradox: only when you accept the reality of your situation can you figure out ways to make things better—and prevent a firing from ever happening again. Here's how one man, working in a highly volatile company in a highly volatile field, uses acceptance as ammunition: "When I come home, I'm totally there for my family. That reinforces the fact that if I get fired, I'd even pump gas to support them. We would survive. I'd never jump out a third-story window. They can threaten to fire me, but my life would be intact."

You might not be able to avoid overattachments to a job, but you can concentrate on the life that's ahead of you—either a new corporate family or a new career. Once you accept your situation, you'll see it more clearly. You'll be able to put a successful job campaign in motion and move on to the best of all possible stages: hope. There *is* a better future waiting.

"WHY DID IT HAPPEN TO ME?"

Getting fired feels awful because it creates so many changes and so many fears. The most common fear is that your career is ruined. The stigma of being fired is no longer what it was. Today it even happens to the most successful people. Remember, Lee Iacocca came to Chrysler because he was fired after thirty-two years with Ford. In fact, recruiter Peter Grimm says that "a growing number of high-powered executives feel if you've never been fired, you haven't been taking enough risk."

You don't have to feel lucky, but you can feel better. Grimm, like most of the executive recruiters I interviewed, takes a very reasonable approach with fired job candidates. "First of all, I look at the kind of company the person worked for and the kind of industry he's in. There are places where firings are common. There are also cases where an organization changed or moved and the person gets caught in the relocation. Those kinds of firings are not going to be held against a person."

Three other common reasons for being fired that *don't* reflect badly on you are:

1. A new boss coming in and forming his own team
2. Budget cuts caused by economic crisis in the firm
3. A merger that creates duplicate staff.

Personality conflicts, corporate culture clashes, and politics also cause many firings. Executive search firms don't just assume you were at fault. People who hire tend to evaluate these reasons according to how many times it's happened. A first-time clash with a difficult boss is usually dismissed as an unfortunate fluke. Similarly, if you were fired because sales were down or you lost your big client, you can use your past successes to demonstrate that this was an isolated, untimely twist of fate. You're only human, and if the problem comes to light, you can confidently reassure the powers that hire that it will never happen again.

Even the very worst situation—fired for cause—does not mean your career is dead. Recruiter Pat Heanue, a search specialist, has seen many careers rebuilt by "people who admit their former problem and emphasize their fervent desire to reestablish their good reputation."

My research and experience bears this out. My files are stuffed with notes and clippings about people who turned seemingly disastrous failures into success.

Think about it. Being fired can be turned into a positive, highly charged challenge. Before you can feel the "rush," you have to understand what you're going through and clear away any doubts that slow you down.

THE FEELINGS ARE THE SAME, BUT THE REASONS ARE DIFFERENT

There are so many reasons for getting fired—and so many waves of bad feelings after it happens. Sometimes it's simply the anger that "they left me before I left them." Sometimes it's a permeating sense of failure. Our pride is hurt. One man who got fired declared that a man "defines the value of his work and himself in terms of money—and he should not. For many men, the slow realization of this fact is some recompense for being let go."

He said more, equally telling and provocative: "There are only two classes of out-of-work men: those who can subsist without a job and those who can't. If you listen to the stories of men in career crises, however, it's as if that distinction did not exist. Those who know they will survive are as fearful as those who think they won't."

Working and making money are basic and important parts of what society says is "masculine." The need to be a good provider is so integral to many a man's self-image that it is not uncommon for them to become sexually impotent after being fired.

Women, on the other hand, do not feel less womanly or feminine if they lose their job. They like to work and earn money as much as men, but it is not intrinsic to their sexual identity. They are more prone to internalize their hurt, blaming *themselves* for "failing." Men tend to chalk it up to an external: a mean boss, circumstance, or fate. They are less likely to see themselves at fault.

Male or female, wrong chemistry or budget cut, the bottom line is that you still got fired. And it doesn't feel good. Once you understand the emotional implications of your new situation, you have to move ahead with the rest of your life. It's time now to find another job—quickly, smoothly, and successfully. It's time to give up that "unrequited love" and find a more fulfilling relationship.

PICKING UP THE PIECES

Here are the answers to five questions most people ask themselves after getting fired:

1. Should I take a vacation?
No. Whether your company has given you two hours to clean out your office or whether you're allowed to stay until you find a new home, almost everyone is tempted to take a vacation. It's the very worst thing you can do. When you first lose a job, your

energies are at fever pitch. You're very geared up. Use that early, strong motivation to get something new going before depression sets in. On the practical side, when your prime source of income has been threatened, it's smart to conserve money and cut unnecessary spending.

Once you are offered another job, you can start working two weeks later. That's when you can enjoy a well-earned vacation— with something to look forward to when you come back!

2. *What kind of severance benefits can I expect?*
Short of blackmail or perpetrating the perfect crime, you should do everything you can to get a good severance package. While a company may not legally owe you anything, most reputable firms feel a moral and ethical obligation to help you over the hump of finding another job. If they don't offer, or if they offer too little, ask, pleasantly but firmly, for what you feel is fair. Outplacement counselors use these rules of thumb: one month of full pay for every $10,000 of annual salary, or two weeks' pay for every year employed. Staying on the payroll is preferable to severance pay as a lump sum. This way your benefits can continue, and if a potential employer checks up on you, it looks as if you're still employed there.

If your company will only give you a lump sum, ask them to continue your medical and life insurance benefits until you have found another home. Ditto with office space and secretarial services. They can help immeasurably in your job search.

Philadelphia outplacement expert K. C. Baldadian says that if you feel you have been unfairly treated, consult a a lawyer familiar with your local laws. Each state has its own guidelines and case law concerning firing. In many states a company can fire you without giving a reason and without any kind of severance pay. They only have to pay you for accrued vacation time. Ms. Baldadian notes, however, that recent court decisions seem to be leaning toward making employers have good cause for termination.

The only situations where you usually have clear legal rights concerning dismissal are those where there is a specific employment contract, or where there has been discrimination on account of age, sex, handicap, or race. But discrimination charges are difficult to prove. Recruiters unanimously agree that you are better off concentrating on a new job rather than looking for redress in the old one.

3. How long will it take me to find a new job?
I've seen people forge straight ahead into the job market full of high hopes only to have them dashed when they didn't find a new job in a couple of weeks. While it is possible to find a new position fast, it's usually more the exception than the norm. Career counselors estimate one month of looking for every $10,000 you make. This means if you were earning $30,000 in your last job, it should take you three months to find a new one. The higher the income, the longer it takes because there are fewer jobs available at the top.

4. How long should I hold out before lowering my horizons?
Since being unemployed is so stressful, and since the longer you are out of work the harder it gets to find a job, I strongly suggest you set a time limit for yourself. Base it on your own stress levels, your financial stability, and the characteristics of the job market in your field. If your time limit passes and you haven't yet found that great job, take *any* decent job. Continue to search for what you want with the security of a regular paycheck coming in.

5. Should I tell people I was fired?
The answer to this classic question depends on your own personality and the situation. The key factor is the way you phrase the "telling." Nothing will clear a crowd faster than announcing, "I've been fired." Most people become uncomfortable. They don't know what to say, so they melt away. Even close friends can avoid you in your time of need, and that can really hurt. On the other hand, saying you're looking for a new job can be a

great conversation starter. A surprising number of people, even relative strangers, will offer suggestions and help. And it definitely doesn't hurt to use *any* contacts you can conjure up.

The best solution is a "cover story," explaining why you left your job without actually coming out and saying you were fired. It's a part of a "gentlemen's agreement"; everyone realizes the truth but acknowledges it silently to avoid embarrassment.

HINTS FROM HINDSIGHT

Basically, looking for a new job after you've been fired involves the same tools as looking for a job while you're still working. Reread Chapter 7, Knowing When It's Time to Go. Go over your Key Benefits List again. List your successes and accomplishments. And above all, keep that confidence level up.

Looking for a new job when you're unemployed does have a few different wrinkles. It's a finer art that requires you to:

- Ditch any victim mentality or false pride that blocks you from using your contacts. Remember that over 60 percent of all jobs come from networking, and you can repay your networking debts later when you're in a position to help others.
- Treat your job search as a full-time job. Use oversize calendars to write in your call-backs under the correct date, and follow up on all leads.
- Prepare yourself for interviews. Memorize your answer to "Tell me why you left." Say what makes you feel most comfortable—but a positive version of the truth is best.
- Check to see if your old boss will give you a good recommendation. Have a friend call and pretend to be a potential employer. If the feedback is bad, you can call the boss and say you'll consult a lawyer if his/her aspersions cause a job-

offer loss. Or, better all around, give potential employers several names to check.

ACTING YOUR WAY
TO A NEW CORPORATE HOME

Take your cue from professional actors. You have a lot in common. Day after day, the actor and the job searcher have to audition for a role they're rarely offered. Both must understand that each director, like each employer, is looking for an idiosyncratic "type." Getting turned down is rarely personal. You have to continue to look for someone who wants your specific kind of background, style, and abilities.

Acknowledge the stress of being unemployed. All too many people take out their frustrations on their spouse or children. Others "medicate" themselves with drugs or booze. Still others keep all the frustrations inside and become so withdrawn that they lose their friends just when they need them most. A professional actor will never get a starring role with that kind of self-destructive behavior—and it can be just as hard for you.

Instead, counteract your frustrations in healthy ways. Take up jogging or any kind of strenuous exercise routine. Talk out your problems with either a professional counselor or a sympathetic friend. Let people give you their support. And do whatever you must to restore your energy and get you back to the work of finding a new job. One woman passed along her coping trick to me: "I'd turn on the shower, get in, and scream at the top of my lungs for a minute or two. It cleansed the spirit along with the body and I was able to get out and make a few more calls."

You will get another job. It's just a matter of time. Your company has divorced you and, yes, that's very traumatic. But I have worked with many clients who have been the victims of corporate divorce and who have suffered the "boot heel in the face." Life looks bleak, but it does get better. It has for them and it can for you.

Let your anger and fear work for you, not against you. Use these emotions to spur you on and keep you "fighting ready" until the right job comes along. Success is always the best revenge.

In time you will find another job, another success. Then you will put aside the pressure of being out of work and go back to the pressures that come with a job, in particular the stress that comes from trying to split your time between your corporate family and your family at home. Let's go on to the very real dilemma of your corporate life versus your personal life. It's all about time. . . .

Chapter 11

Bigamy: Corporate Life Versus Personal Life

"There's just enough energy left to flick on the TV and crawl into bed."   —Junior executive,
                        Major broadcasting corporation

"George never gets to see the baby. He gets home at eight o'clock—just when the baby is going to sleep."

"I'm always under pressure. Something's got to give."

"I want it all—career, marriage, and family."

Do any of these sound familiar? They should. They're all part of the quandary each of us has faced at one time or another in our lives. There never seems to be enough time to spend on the things we want—with time left over for us and us alone.

The time pressure cooker makes some of us divorce a corporation just to get a breather. The fast-paced race makes others ignore the real needs of friends and lovers, children and mates. The only way to satisfy all the demands of our corporate family without cheating our natural one is to take a hard, realistic look at ourselves. It all comes down to time. . . .

CONTROLLING THE CLOCK

Almost as much has been written about time as love, death, and sunrise. It's the stuff of riddles and the essence of poetry. It is undeniably our most valuable commodity. We can never get enough to do everything we want.

To be successful in the corporate world as well as in your personal life, you have to analyze what you need for your unique version of "the good life." Behind every successful person is an ability to manage time.

It boils down to a question of choice. What are your true inner needs? For some people it's easy to choose work over personal nirvana. Writer/scientist Isaac Asimov says, "I don't go on vacation. You see, a vacation is doing what you want to do and to stop doing what you have to do. But I like what I do, so I'm on vacation 365 days a year. If I had to play volleyball or fish, that would be the real work."

For others, spending lots of time away from work is the key to happiness. "I can leave work and be really happy with myself," says one middle manager. "I don't need work to define myself. I like to have time to discover the world, to let experiences sink in."

But for many of us, the choice is muddled. The pressure builds. We tend to balance so much that we become expert acrobats, always under constant strain that the entire act will come tumbling down on top of us. Listen to what a hard-working office manager told me: "I'm frantic every morning. It's real hard on me. My husband and I even take showers together because there's no time for separate ones. Every morning we have coffee and I'm screaming at him to get into the car to make the train. We're down to the wire every day. We just make it as the train pulls in." And the pace doesn't quit until she falls asleep each night.

Industrial psychologists recently reported that many corporate managers are disillusioned. While getting their degrees, they en-

155

visioned pushing their chairs back, putting their feet up on the desk, and gazing into the future, planning strategy. Instead they find themselves in jobs with so many phone calls, so many projects, and so many pressures that they feel like jugglers rather than strategists.

Let's face it. The eight-hour day is a thing of the past. Everyone is watching the bottom line, and there's enormous pressure to produce. The competition is always intense, competition from within your company and from outside the company for your markets or mastery. Escalating salaries make companies want more value for the money.

All this translates into more time spent with the corporate family . . . and less time at home. This time pressure can be found in every field in every area, from corporate boardrooms to research labs. As one research scientist told me, "I'm always under this terrible time pressure. If I don't spend enough time testing my results, they'll be disproven and I'll be discredited. But if I spend too much time, then someone else will publish the results first." He works late every night, always trying to squeeze in "a little more time."

At least this scientist loves what he does. Sometimes we hate the task at hand so much that we'll spend more time avoiding it than doing it, taking twice the time to finish. In fact, the cruelest irony of them all is that people who dislike their jobs often have the greatest time pressures. As one salesman told me, "I feel like I've been working all day, when I haven't done anything except procrastinate."

There's a way to avoid this syndrome. If you don't like your job, but you can't leave because it's a part of your "five-year plan," you must schedule free time for positive reinforcement. Whether a round of golf or a trip to a museum, a reward after your hard work will make you feel less like a grind. On the other hand, if you're more like Isaac Asimov and you love your work, you have to be strong enough to ignore what other people say. Think of yourself and what you want.

The demands of time are different for different people. Single or married, male or female, childless or parent of three, personal-time advocate or workaholic master, each has its own set of variables . . . and its own special time warp.

Time Warp 1:

SINGLE AND FREE

That's what they say. And it's partially true. You're free to stay as long as you want at your corporate home because there's no one at your other home to answer to. But as anyone who is single can tell you, those nights alone get pretty lonely. Relationships with another person take time to build. When you're working hard to pay your own way, you can get disillusioned and fall into an "Is That All There Is?" syndrome. If you absolutely love your work and feel no need for a personal life, fine. But if you want some free time to meet someone—or simply enjoy some hours of solitude away from your desk—you need to make that time. An account executive at an investment house said: "After my divorce I knew I'd have to work hard to get ahead. I used to feel awful when some guy called me up for a date and I had to say no because of work. But work was important for my self-esteem—and my rent—and I turned those phone calls around to my advantage. If a guy didn't understand my work habits, I figured he was someone I wouldn't have wanted to go out with anyway. And if he understood, then I'd make the time to see him later in the week."

Time Warp 2:

I DO, I DO . . . I THINK

Two might live more cheaply than one, but timewise the cost is more dear. You already have the relationship, but you have to make the time to enjoy it. As one senior vice-president told me, "My wife and I make appointments to see each other." It sounds cold, but it is practical. As with singles, romance must be scheduled, whether it's candlelight dinners for two on Friday night or Sundays in bed with the answering machine on. John Foster of Boyden Associates says, "The biggest social and cultural change I've seen is the two-career family. Many couples under forty-five are extremely career dependent. It's a definite partnership."

In fact, some corporations now pay commuting costs for the spouse when couples must live apart in different cities because of their careers. Couples will devote weekdays totally to their jobs and spend weekends together.

Time management becomes even more important when children are involved, but before discussing this vital issue, I'd like to talk about the not-so-obvious differences between women and men. . . .

Time Warp 3:

I AM WOMAN

Regardless of what we think intellectually, there are ingrained societal beliefs that separate women from men, beliefs that add so much pressure that they've led many a woman to divorce her corporation or an entire career.

The need to be attractive and social are two such pressures women still feel even when they reach the very top. Listen to what a noted cancer researcher and department head at a major hospital was quoted as saying: "Research is such a competitive field, and most of my colleagues are men who have wives to do everything at home. I know if I have to give a dinner for a hundred people and I have to be dressed and get my hair done, I can't concentrate on my work."

Women have also been taught to think differently about the priorities of work life versus home life. In the classic study by

Matina Horner, most people predicted that top female medical student "Anne" would have a miserable personal life. But the group expected top male medical student "John" to be extremely happy. When Anne's story was changed to say she'd graduated in the top half of her class, she was expected to live happily. John, however, was considered a failure because he was "only" in the top half. It's ingrained beliefs like this that pressure Anne to take a maternity leave after the baby is born and John to work ten-hour days and rarely see his children.

However, things are changing. A recent study asked 1500 middle and top managers, both male and female, which gave them more satisfaction: home or work. Sixty percent of the women chose *work,* but only 37 percent of the men made the same choice. The study found that women managers were more willing to work longer hours, relocate, and change their life-style's for a better-paying job.

And women *have* to be serious about their careers. Not only because they like to work as much as men do, but because divorce, desertion, or widowhood will force 85 percent of all American women to support themselves (and often their children) at some point in their lives.

Time Warp 4:

I AM MAN

Studies show that women have taken on career responsibilities for their corporate family faster than men have accepted household responsibilities for the nuclear family. Women realize that a career doesn't cost them their feminity, but men, on the whole, have a hard time accepting the fact that household chores will *not* make them appear any less manly. As a psychologist with a corporate advisory service says, "Unless he's very innovative and unusual, the man's not going to be the one who initiates housework. He might complain, 'I don't know how you live in this pigsty,' but he won't pick up the broom first."

Men might not be initiating the housework, but they *are* doing the chores more and more. The results of a national survey conducted by the University of Michigan showed a 20 percent increase in the number of hours men spent on childcare and housework from 1965 to 1981. During the same period the number of hours women under forty-five put into their home decreased by 30 percent.

What kind of chores are men doing? Researchers at Cunningham & Walsh, an advertising agency, found that husbands are assuming many of the traditional homemaking chores for their working wives: 70 percent cook, 49 percent vacuum, 41 percent do the dishes, and 56 percent shop. But 75 percent of the husbands who buy the groceries only buy what their wives tell them to buy. Women still have the overall responsibility of organizing what needs to be done, of running the household.

Regardless of who's doing what, time pressure is an equal opportunity problem. With wives devoting more time to their corporate family and men devoting more time to the family chores, there's less and less free time to savor life's pleasures. While racing down the supermarket aisles after a grueling day at the office, what man *or* woman hasn't been tempted to chuck it all and grab the next plane to Tahiti? And the pressure only mounts when . . .

Time Warp 5:

BABY MAKES THREE

I remember the story a division head of a pharmaceutical firm told me when she got pregnant: "I told my supervisor that I wanted to take three months off to have my baby. He said, 'It's so unfortunate that women have to drop out to become mothers.' I replied: 'Yes, it's true, but I work twice as hard as the men here, so I feel I'm entitled to three months off!' "

This woman had no doubts about what she wanted and she had no guilt. Many women are not that lucky. They are wracked with confusion and guilt over the King Solomon choice between being corporate mother or earth mother.

Ironically, it's the number of options available today that makes the decision so difficult. For all the talk about househusbands, it is still very hard to find one. But it's still quite acceptable for a woman to divorce her corporation to be a mother. It's also acceptable to arrange a "trial separation"—a maternity leave— for up to a year. At the same time, it's common to see women practically take a taxi from the delivery room back to their desks. What's a mother to do?

Get out your benefits cards and sort out your *Very Important, Moderately Important,* and *Not Important* piles one more time. Do your *Very Important* cards look like the priorities of a full-time parent, a full-time career person, or a person who tries to cut the difference? The choice to make is there, and each choice has its own pleasures and compromises.

If you opt for full-time motherhood, chances are you won't know for sure if you've made the right choice until the baby's home and the initial confusion has settled down—even if you have unquestioning faith in your convictions. When you've divorced your career to stay home with baby, there's going to be culture shock, a loss of income, and, unfortunately, a loss of self-esteem. Unless you're talking to other mothers, saying "I'm a mother" at parties just isn't going to have the same impact as mentioning the business role you once had. I strongly advise even the most committed full-time mother to keep her skills up. Read the trade papers. Take courses. Go to seminars. Even though raising a baby can be a full-time job, it's important to keep your options open just in case. . . .

When it comes to options, most women still choose the "trial separation," taking anywhere from three months to three years before going back to work. Timing here can be crucial. Planning when to have children can mean the difference between keeping your career on an even keel—or getting way off the track. Recruiters have two schools of thought here, both plausible. You can either have your children before you start a serious career path, entering the work force at, say, twenty-five or twenty-seven, *or* you can build up a career, take a maternity leave in your mid-thirties, then come back where you left off. But you have to plan your strategy just right. As one recruiter points out, "It can be very destructive if management knows you're going to do it. And taking a long maternity leave can make people respect you less."

Unfortunately, I've found this to be true. Time and time again senior managers tell me that "Women with children are very distracted." Being a mother can stop the promotions from coming in if you work for a company that firmly believes motherhood belongs at home.

Even if your corporate family supports your pregnancy, there will still be sacrifices to be made, especially if you decide to take one to three years off. You may have to return at a lower level. A recruiter explained: "A one-year leave can very seriously hurt your climb. Your position will be changed. People who make long-term plans for promotions will see your priorities as time off versus a career." One way to combat this kind of thinking is to move to a company where promotions are given for achievement, not longevity or long hours. If you work hard and seize opportunities, you just might be able to jump over everybody else.

No matter what choice you ultimately make, as a new mother it's going to be hard not to feel guilty when you kiss your baby good-bye, attaché case in hand. Our duties as mothers and fathers are inbred in us from the day we are born. Men are "supposed" to earn the money to take care of the children. Mothers are "supposed" to take care of the rest. No one expects a father to be home with the kids. In fact, when a man does take over some of these responsibilities, he's warmly praised for being a great father. But women will only hear criticism if they *don't* do their nurturing as if it were second nature.

The guilt does work both ways. "Many men have a deep fear of being ridiculed by their colleagues if they relieve their wives of childcare duties," says Dr. Richard Stevenson, Jr., a psychologist in charge of the fathers' groups at the Bank Street School in Manhattan. He told me about one particular manager who was in charge of scheduling hours for his sales force. In order to plan for the next day's work, he held a group meeting at the end of each day. This man also happened to love picking his daughter up at school, cooking dinner with her, and chatting before his wife came home from work. But he was embarrassed to tell his sales group that he wanted to leave early. Instead he'd say that his wife and daughter were twisting his arm. He *had* to leave by 5:15 or he'd have hell to pay that night. But after working with Dr. Stevenson, he realized he was doing not only his wife and daughter a disservice, but himself as well. He told his sales force the truth. And rather than elbow-jabs and snickers, he received respect. All the men appreciated the fact that he wanted to be a good father.

There are solutions to ease the guilt and make bringing up baby compatible with bringing home the bacon. Here are a few that corporate men and women have used with success:

1. *Work out an agreement in writing* that divides the household responsibilities between the two of you. Remember that the most important "household duty" is spending time enjoying each other and the baby. Try to avoid as much drudgery as you can. Your world won't fall apart if dust balls gather in your living room corners, but it *will* fall apart if time pressures build up and hurt your marriage or your child.
2. *Make children part of the household team* by giving them small chores as soon as possible. Praise their skills and effort. They'll be able to see their chores as a contribution, some-

163

thing good for the whole family. Everyone—even the kids —is pitching in and having fun. The same team spirit that keeps corporate families together can be used at home.

3. *Bring your children into your corporate world.* Mary Kay's son describes his Saturday afternoons: "While we were growing up, the other kids on the block were mowing lawns for money. But in our house, we were packing Mother's orders to be delivered. At the end of the day, I remember talking about how much money we earned. Could *we* go to the movies? Can *we* go out to eat?" It will help bring your two worlds closer together.

4. *Share the mothering and the fathering.* If corporate success is extremely important to both of you, this is a fact that must be accepted: women cannot be both corporate mother and earth mother at the same time. In fact, the most committed corporate parents I know function like two very loving fathers—with a babysitter taking up the slack.

THE CORPORATE FAMILY
VERSUS THE NATURAL FAMILY

Mother or father, being a part of a working parent team is not a bad thing. Forget the vacuuming. Forget that you've already eaten hamburgers three nights this week. When you come home from your office, you're home. You're together as a family. Enjoy and relish your time together.

And remember, too, that nothing is irrevocable. Later on, you might feel as this executive did: "I decided I was paying too much to be at the top. I was simply putting in too many long hours. When my husband bought my twelve-year-old daughter her first bra, I couldn't stand it. I felt I was missing too much of my children's lives. I quit."

I did the same. In 1969 I received an offer to work for one of the best management consulting companies in the country. It would have meant ten-hour days and extensive travel. I wanted to have children, and I realized I wouldn't be able to be with them as much as I would like. I couldn't be the mother I wanted to be and a top consultant too. Instead I became a psychologist, which gave me the flexible hours I needed to spend time with my children.

Many men told me their world opened up after their children were born. In their desire to be at home with their families, long hours at the office became a thing of the past. They began to see something more in life than just work. Others made the opposite switch. They became more dedicated to work in their new roles of parent and provider.

Each of us has to find a balance between home and office, based on our personal values and life situation. There is no one right choice. Obviously, it is possible to combine a demanding full-time career and parenthood. And the ability to earn a living and juggle several different roles promotes a tremendous sense of well-being among women in mid-life, according to a study done at Brandeis University.

But juggling can be exhausting, and the time pressures on a juggler are enormous. A deputy director of a large public service organization says, "I have time for myself only when I stay up until four A.M. and put on a record and try to remember who I am. I'm paying the price of combining my career with mother-hood and marriage. But I think people have the right to do what they do best. I think I have a right to choose to work *and* have a family."

With careful time management, however, this woman is suc-ceeding at both. She's been known to interrupt a dinner meeting to go to a pay phone and read a chapter from her son's latest bedtime story. And nine times a year she takes a hookey day and does something special with her son.

We are learning to adapt. The *versus* between our corporate family and our natural one is slowly turning to *and*. Women are spending more time on the job and men are spending more time at home . . . and at some point down the road, their shifting roles will meet. When I asked my thirteen-year-old son—the one who's learning to bake cookies and sew on buttons in school—how a mother's responsibilities are different from a father's, his quick reply was: "The mother feeds the kids and takes care of them. The father earns the money." But when I went to my five-year-old daughter—the one who wants to be president of the United States—and asked her the same question, she thought about it a moment and said, "They're the same."

Time Warp 6:

I AM A WORKAHOLIC

There are two types of workaholics: the healthy ones and the unhealthy ones. The healthy ones love their work. Healthy workaholics also enjoy their play, their money, their sex, and good health. They are relatively trouble-free. As one successful man said: "Work is only work if you'd rather be doing something else."

An unhealthy workaholic, on the other hand, is a prime candidate for a "Type A" heart attack. You've seen them: always doing two or more things at once while jiggling their legs and fingers. They're easily aroused, compulsive to the point of obsession, and usually sitting on the edge of their chair. One "Type A" workaholic bitterly said to me, "Work isn't fun. If I was having fun, I'd go play golf." But he spends twelve-hour days at work and spends the rest of his time doing chores. In his classic "Type A" style, he gets "tee'd off"—but never on the green.

There are corporations or bosses that demand workaholic hours. These are places where you are suspect if you use all your vacation days, where anyone who leaves before 8:00 P.M. is not considered serious about a career. Unless you are in that kind of culture, the good news is that taking time away from your corporate family will not, in most cases, hurt your career. A study of

2,400 IBM managers showed that there was no correlation *what-soever* between effectiveness ratings and the amount of time they worked over and above the obligatory forty-hour week. (The average amount of hours worked in the study was actually fifty a week.) Putting in late hours has its place, but unless your corporate culture demands them, arduous nights at your desk may not only cost you your personal life, but the respect of your supervisor as well. As one senior manager told me, "People who always stay late or work every weekend are not handling their tasks efficiently."

On the other hand, all work and no play doesn't necessarily make every person dull. The first thing you have to determine is whether you love your hard work—or hate it. One of my clients, a single woman who loved her demanding job, began questioning her long hours when everyone around her started telling her she *had* to have some free time. They decided it wasn't healthy for her to work so much. But after she made her Key Benefits List, she discovered that the most important hooks for her were "Prestige of the Organization," "Power," and "Challenge." Low on her list were "Personal Style" and "Family Life." For this woman, the long hours and hard work were vital for her sense of well-being—though she is learning to schedule in some relaxation time.

BEING MARRIED TO SOMEONE
WHO IS MARRIED TO THE COMPANY

What if your problem is being married to a workaholic? This is usually a condition that affects the wife rather than the other way around, though that too is changing.

It's tough to keep your anger and frustration in check when, say, during a family outing, your husband leaves you and the kids in the car "just to run up to the office and fetch some papers"—only to return four hours later!

167

More than one woman told me a story like this, and there's only one moral I could give them: don't allow yourself to be in a position where you have to wait. Make your plans and have your husband come to the dinner party or the weekend retreat when he's through with work. In a study conducted among 150 "power widows," a group of women married to superachievers, a good deal of anger and frustration at their husband's long work days and prolonged absences was found—to no one's surprise. But the findings indicated that the marriages remained stable if the women were able to maintain a positive attitude.

In World War II, for instance, husbands were away for very long stretches at a time. But their wives viewed the absence as a good and important duty—and portrayed it to their children as such. Very few children were emotionally harmed.

The same still holds true today. One woman married to a workaholic tells her kids that "their father is working at his job so we can live this way. We live very well and the kids understand this. They're proud of the way he handles responsibility."

She has also discussed the situation with her workaholic husband, and he has learned to manage his time with both his corporate family and his real one. "If things are really important at home," he told me, "I do it. And I will take getting home on time over a crisis at the office if we've planned something together or it's a school function. But I'm careful to only promise to do things that I think are important—and ninety-nine percent of the time I will honor that promise to my wife and kids."

The key to changing disruptive workaholic behavior—as well as make for a better life in any of the "time warps"—is to manage your time.

TIME MANAGEMENT TECHNIQUES

A personal life can have a place side by side with your corporate life. Here's how:

1. Make a list of your goals. This way you'll know what's important to you—and you'll be able to allocate time to achieve them.

2. Don't devote big effort to tasks of little value. This works at home and on the job. Don't bother traveling to three different supermarkets, coupons in hand. Don't bother sending a memo when a quick phone call will do. And delegate anything you don't have to do personally.

3. Schedule time for family, fun, and relaxation. It's a good use of time. By relaxing, you'll come back refreshed and ready to work—and you'll do a better job.

4. Make a "to do" list every day. What's not done is either forgotten because it's *not* important, or it's rolled over to the next day's list.

5. Change your thinking from what can I do to what can I NOT do. It will help you understand exactly what your priorities are.

6. Remember this important time management insight: the 80/20 rule. It might help you set priorities:

- 80% of your money comes from 20% of your assignments
- 80% of your orders comes from 20% of your customers
- 80% of your fun comes from 20% of your friends
- 80% of your value comes from 20% of the things you do

7. Take a tip from successful executives. The way they behave leads to good time management—instinctively. Research shows:

- They think more in terms of tasks accomplished than hours spent.
- They delegate as many important tasks, not just the trivial ones, as they can.
- They do not overplan, but approach important tasks with a general strategy, assuming that decisions will become clear as events unfold.
- They disavow hard-nosed attitudes such as "You're paid to work *not* to enjoy it."

169

Think smart. Your corporate life and your personal life do not have to be at war. Time waits for no man, but no man—or woman—need wait for time. You can do everything you want (or at least 80 percent) right now.

Epilogue

The Great Paradox—
To Avoid Divorce . . .
Prepare for It

"To become part of the top brass you have to live, breathe, and think the company."   —Owner, Executive search firm

versus

"Never, never get yourself in a position where you emotionally or financially *need* your job—it leaves you wide open for abuse."   —Senior manager, Fortune 100 company

After having spent nearly three years researching this book, I decided it was time to stop. I had interviewed over one hundred people, and while each had an interesting story or two to share, no one was telling me anything new anymore.

Yet I couldn't resist going to just one more conference. This one was on managerial team building. Executives were flying in from all over the country to attend it. While it added a few new twists, the underlying philosophy at the conference held the same enlightened approach I had heard from other experts:

- To meet the challenges of rapidly changing markets, companies have to make their white-collar employees more productive, loyal, and creative; team building helps accomplish this.

- The best people are going to stay at a company that gives them financial rewards plus the psychological rewards gained from being a part of a challenging, simpatico team.
- Generating team spirit will encourage a healthy dual loyalty —commitment to both the individual's professional growth and the growth of the organization as a whole.

On the last day of the conference, several of us enjoyed a lunch break on the hotel terrace. My companions, all managers with well-known corporations, were Organization Men 1980s style. Each one clearly felt a part of the corporate family. And all had happily given up their weekend to come to this conference in the hopes of learning something productive they could bring back home. They spoke proudly of "my" company and "our" way of doing things, and had a fervent desire to make their corporations grow.

And yet when one of these managers asked me what I did, the conversation shifted gears. "I'm writing a book on why it's so hard to leave a job, why people get stuck, even in jobs they hate . . ." I began—and watched as an electric charge went through the group. Each one of these loyal, committed managers suddenly began to talk at once. Everyone had a story to tell about a friend, or a friend of a friend, who'd gotten stuck in a job, who'd stayed on way past the time they should have left. Then, as trust began to build, they began to share the fears that they had themselves, that this might happen to them too someday. They'd thought about it, but they'd never vocalized it before. In private, some of them had secretly built up strategies to avoid ever ending up as deadwood. Under the Indian summer sun, they talked about those strategies. . . .

"You need an odd combination of trust and caution—trusting the company and being trusted, but having everyone sense that you're not going to be jerked around," one of the managers, a woman, said. "You have to buy the team approach. But if you buy it completely, you won't be valued. I'm loyal, friendly, and committed, but I'm never going to stay in a bad situation and just complain. I always remember that everyone is dispensable. And I keep myself financially able to move on."

"Yeah," agreed the youngest manager. "The vast majority of people I know live up to their last dollar. Then they only have the opportunity to move immediately to something good or better. I know I can leave any time because I have my bail-out account with my bail-out amount in it. I never want to use it, but I know it's there and it maintains my attitude: step on me and I won't be here."

"You've got to sit loose in the saddle," added the graying personnel manager. "A company senses when people will never leave and it develops contempt for them. I hear people say, 'I'd never leave. I don't know where I'd go. Who would have me?' You should never feel that! And if you feel it, *never* admit it! It's asking for trouble."

Everyone nodded in agreement. After a brief pause, he continued: "All my life I deferred to authority, but as I got older I developed a sense of mortality. I decided that before my life is over, more of my choices are going to be mine. Otherwise life wouldn't be worthwhile. I lost a job a few years ago and I discovered that life didn't fall apart. Now I keep myself independent by making sure I always have other options. I'd hate to leave my company, but if I did . . . I would survive."

At this point the managers were leaning forward to catch every word. There was a mixture of relief and interest on each face. There was a sense of intimacy that transcended the previous conversations about the conference. Here they were, talking about the most private professional issues in public, and each one immediately understood. There was an urgent feeling in the air to get things off their chests . . . at last.

As I sat there, scribbling down their words as fast as I could, I was surprised to find three people in one place who had such definite plans to remain committed to their corporate families, but free to leave if they had to. I also thought of all the people I had talked to who had gotten panicky when their careers hit snags, the people who didn't feel they had any options, no room to escape. And I wondered. Would the bail-out account be used if an insolvable problem occurred? Or would that man, even with the power of his savings to back him up, stay in a situation that bled him into deadwood?

My ruminations were interrupted by a man at the next table who had overheard us. I'd spoken to him before, and I remembered him saying that he got up every morning at six to squeeze in some extra time at the office, and that his wife didn't see him for days on end when he was involved in a special project at work. In fact, he'd seemed so utterly immersed in his career that I was amazed when he grabbed a chair, sat down, and said, "I made a conscious decision never to be married to the company. Once you get an emotional mind-set that it's something more than a job or income, you are psychologically married. Then you get worried that you've got this thing to protect. It's absolutely foolish to get emotionally involved in any company unless you own it. I keep a part of myself separate: I never mix business with pleasure. Family with business."

We were all listening. No one interrupted. And no one noticed that almost everyone else on that terrace had gone back in. He continued: "I have a high work ethic. I work hard, I've got a good title, and I'm happy. But I never turn down a call from a headhunter. If anything goes wrong, I can leave. I warn myself daily it's not important. Like the Roman generals who kept their heads by having their slaves whisper in their ears: 'It's not important. It's not important.' "

A job. A title. Security. Success. They're all so terribly important—and yet this man is right. There is a paradox here. To keep your head, you have to be able to lose your job. When a mistake or a problem or simply a bad twist of fate throws up a roadblock, the only way to attack it with perspective is to know you don't *have* to: you *choose* to. The only way to decide rationally whether to stay on and fight or to make an orderly retreat is to know that you have the option to go.

Over and over again I have found that managers who successfully move on to greener pastures and managers who stay with their company and rebuild shattered careers are those who have carefully nurtured their ability to leave. They decide to stay because they *want* to, not because they *have* to. It makes all the difference in the world.

Psychologists find this same paradox existing in healthy marriages. In a good marriage, each partner leans on the other. But only a person who feels independent can be dependent without becoming utterly submerged. Even in the best marriages, a person who becomes too dependent, too needy, often stops expecting respect. They lose their own identity. Only people who know they can survive alone can risk being rejected—by standing up for their rights and demanding respect.

So it is with corporate families. To be able to love a corporate home in a self-respecting manner requires—paradoxically—the ability to leave it if worst comes to worst.

Well-run corporations understand this dual loyalty. It's the way they operate. When an employee joins the firm, everyone hopes it will be " 'til death do us part." But even the most paternalistic companies that hired for life, places like "Father Yellow" Kodak, had large layoffs when profits were squeezed in the '80s. Any executive who thinks he is wedded for life to his corporate home can find himself the victim of unrequited love if the corporation can cut its losses or gain more profit by letting him go. That's just business. A company's first loyalty has to be to stockholders' profits—not personnel.

Executives managing the business of their personal careers may have to make similar choices. If a job change holds the likely promise of cutting their psychological losses or boosting their personal profits, executives have to think of themselves first. And there may be no other choice but divorce.

175

But divorce is painful . . . and often unnecessary. To be loyal to yourself, you should try to work things out at home first. More and more people seem to be doing just that. Commitment seems to be making a comeback. The divorce rate for marriage is beginning to ebb. Similarly, the wild job-hopping of the 1970s and early '80s seems to be cooling. Only a few years ago, M.B.A.s who stayed with even a good company for five or—God forbid —ten years were considered stagnant. Now those same M.B.A.s would be considered lucky. And they make their luck by loving their company—but loving themselves more.

The sun was beginning to set. The breeze grew chilly. But here, light years away from the corporate skyscrapers and crowded city streets, we continued to talk about our lives and our loyalties until it grew late.

I was glad I had come, because the conference had helped cement in my mind what this book is all about: us. All of us who have ever worked in an organization, who have ever felt happily attached or locked in a trap. It is all about knowing when to leave home to continue growing and when to stay put and work things out. In learning about the loyalty that's bred in our corporate families, we should learn more about loyalty to ourselves.

And that's the bottom line.

Notes

Notes

4   2. Terrence Deal and Allen Kennedy. *Corporate Cultures.*

5   3. Robert Levering, Milton Moskowitz, and Michael Katz. *The 100 Best Companies to Work for in America.*

6   4. Happy workaholics: Jane Brody. "Workaholism." Marilyn Machlowitz. *Workaholics.*

12   5. It's clear that the vast majority of Fortune 500 CEOs are one- or two-company men, but the actual percentage varies according to the study: Malcolm Carter. "The Ins and Outs of Switching Jobs." Ann Morrison. "Job Hopping to the Top."

Chapter 2

22   1. Office manager story: interviews and an adaptation from Earl Shorris. *The Oppressed Middle.*

23   2. Leavitt quotes about the manipulative boss: Harold Leavitt. *Managerial Psychology.*

Chapter 3

30   1. The AT&T study: Roy Rowan. "Rekindling Corporate Loyalty."

Chapter 4

40   1. Ouchi quote: William Ouchi. *Theory Z.*

41   2. Drucker quote: Peter Drucker. "Thomas Watson's Principles of Modern Management."

41   3. *The 100 Best Companies to Work for in America* stresses the importance of making employees feel like part of a team or family.

42   4. Hawthorne studies: F. J. Roethlisberger and W. J. Dickson. *Management and the Worker.*

42   5. Herzberg findings: Frederick Herzberg. "One More Time: How Do You Motivate Employees?"

Notes

42 6. Existential dualism: Ernest Becker. *The Denial of Death*. Cited and discussed by Thomas Peters and Robert Waterman in *In Search of Excellence*.

Chapter 5

61 1. Mobility of men with working versus nonworking wives: Marta Mooney. "Does It Matter if His Wife Works?"

62 2. Positive and negative effects of a move on children: interview with Dr. Stephen Eliot and "Changing Schools: It Can Hurt."

Chapter 6

74 1. Money is the prime motivator: interviews and Gary Dessler. *Personnel Management*.

74 2. Amounts of raises: interviews and "Have Talent, Will Travel."

74 3. Job-stayers earn more than job-hoppers: J. Sterling Livingston. "The Troubled Transition." Gerard Roche. "Compensation and the Mobile Executive."

75 4. Merck study: William Serrin. "Unions in Merck Strike Try to Involve the Public."

75 5. Wang: Fox Butterfield. "Chinese Immigrant Emerges as Boston's Top Benefactor."

76 6. Security from promoting from within at J. C. Penney: Donald Siebert and William Proctor. *The Ethical Executive*.

78 7. Giving people visibility instead of a raise: Mortimer Feinberg. *Effective Psychology for Managers*.

78 8. Family attachment: interviews and Landon Jones. "The Mid-Career Switch."

82 9. DeVries: James Barron. "Humana Focus: Technology."

82 10. Superbrokers: Leslie Wayne. "The Method and Magic of the Superbroker."

84 11. Trammell Crow: Charlotte Curtis. "The Dallas Billionaires."

Chapter 7

92 1. 80 percent of job changers think they are getting a promotion: John Veiga. "Do Managers on the Move Get Anywhere?"

92 2. Only one in five changes jobs successfully: Malcolm Carter. "The Ins and Outs of Switching Jobs."

101 3. 64 percent of senior vice-presidents were helped by mentors: from a study conducted by the search firm Heidrick and Struggles cited by Donald Siebert and William Proctor in *The Ethical Executive*.

101 4. The similarity of successful and derailed executives: Morgan McCall, Jr., and Michael Lombardo. "What Makes a Top Executive?"

102 5. "Meet your failures head-on": Paul Ray, Sr. "How Not to Get Fired."

105 6. Only one in twenty middle managers makes it to top management: Daniel Levinson. *The Seasons of a Man's Life*.

105 7. The average CEO's term is seven years: cited in interviews with recruiters.

106 8. Executive I.Q.: Daniel Goleman. "Successful Executives Rely on Own Kind of Intelligence."

Chapter 8

110 1. "Just like in a love relationship . . .": Robin Reif. "Breaking Up (With Your Job) Is Hard to Do."

110 2. ". . . fifty ways to leave your lover": Landon Jones. "The Mid-Career Switch."

114 3. 60 percent of jobs found through networking: Joie Smith. "Focus on Goals, Skills, and Accomplishments."

115 4. Want ad statistics: Richard Bolles. *What Color Is Your Parachute?*

Notes

115 5. Thirty seconds per résumé: estimates from interviews.

117 6. Job hunters make twenty-five to fifty contacts per week: Daniel Knowles. "Stress Versatility and Uniqueness to Generate Interviews."

118 7. Five stages of an interview adapted from: John Arnold. *Shooting the Executive Rapids*.

Chapter 9

126 1. ". . . smitten on the road to Damascus": Landon Jones. "The Mid-Career Switch."

129 2. Scrabble producer: Walter Waggoner. "James Brunot, 82, The First Producer of Scrabble Games."

129 3. Cuisinart: Susan Anderson. "Starting Over: Life After Retirement."

129 4. Bloomingdale's: "President Resigns at Bloomingdale's."

135 5. Atari quote: John Merwin. "Have You Got What It Takes?"

135 6. McKinsey study: Arthur Howe. "Entrepreneurial Profiles."

136 7. Eight out of ten fail in three years: William Zucker. "Starting Your Own Business."

Chapter 10

140 1. Percentage ever fired: Tom Biracree. *How You Rate: Men*.

140 2. Six stages of emotion first formulated by Elisabeth Kübler-Ross, *On Death and Dying*.

145 3. Liz Peer story: Gwenda Blair. "The Heart of the Matter."

147 4. A man defines his value in terms of money quotes: Robert Capon. "Being Let Go."

Note: Various rules of thumb and pieces of advice cited in this chapter were shared by executive recruiters, employment agency owners, and outplacement specialists. Sometimes they gave conflicting pieces of advice, which just shows that there are no hard-and-fast rules in the difficult process of job change. Two people who were especially generous with their time and expertise were K. C. Baldadian, of Integra, Inc., in Philadelphia, and Collette Conroy, on staff in outplacement with a Fortune 500 firm in New York.

Chapter 11

155 1. Asimov quote: Max Millard. "Isaac Asimov: West Side Workaholic."

155 2. Managers feel like jugglers: I wish that I could give credit for these ideas, which I heard in a presentation at the American Psychological Association convention held in New York a few years ago. I have lost the notes I took there and do not know which of the various talks by industrial psychologists contained these insights.

159 3. Anne, the top medical student: Matina Horner and Mary Walsh. "Psychological Barriers to Success in Women."

159 4. Anne, in the top half of the class: Michele Paludi. "Horner Revisited: How Successful Must Anne and John Be Before Fear of Success Sets In?"

159 5. Women are more dedicated and satisfied at work than at home: Warren Schmidt and Barry Posner. *Managerial Values and Perspectives.*

159 6. 85 percent will be self-supporting: Julia Scott. "Women in the Work Force."

159 7. Men won't initiate housework: Jean Grasso Fitzpatrick. "The Dirty Truth About Housework."

160 8. Michigan housework study reported in: Daniel Goleman. "As Sex Roles Change, Men Turn to Therapy to Cope with Stress."

160 9. Percentage of men who do housework: Leslie Gevirtz. "You Need a Man Around the House."

161 10. In 1975 a national survey found that 75 percent of all women want to work, but want to take a few years off when their children are young: National Commission on the Observance of International Women's Year. *To Form a More Perfect Union*.

164 11. Mary Kay Ash's son: Kathy LaTour. "What Motivates Mary Kay?"

165 12. Brandeis study: Grace Baruch, Rosalind Barnett, and Caryl Rivers. *Lifeprints*.

165 13. Time alone at four A.M. quote: Kay Holmes. "Working Wife and House Husband."

166 14. Healthy workaholics: Jane Brody. "Workaholism." Marilyn Machlowitz. *Workaholics*.

166 15. "Work is only work . . .": Charlotte Curtis. "A Tycoon with a New Bank."

166 16. Unhealthy workaholics: Jane Brody. "Modifying 'Type A' Behavior Reduces Heart Attacks."

167 17. IBM study: An unpublished internal study done at IBM and discussed with an IBM spokesman. I initially read about it in Jean Grasso Fitzpatrick's "Stop Working Late."

168 18. Power widows: Annie Moldafsky. "How 'Power Widows' Feel About Success." Frances Bremer and Emily Vogl. *Coping with His Success*.

168 19. World War II insight: Interview with Dr. Richard Stevenson.

169 20. 80/20 rule: Alan Lakein. *How to Get Control of Your Time and Your Life*.

169 21. Successful executive style: Daniel Goleman. "Successful Executives Rely on Own Kind of Intelligence."

Epilogue

175 1. "Father Yellow" firings: Eric Berg. "Shrinking a Staff the Kodak Way."

176 2. Lower divorce rate: "U.S. Divorces Fell in '82; First Decline in 20 Years."

Bibliography

Adams, Jane. *Making Good*. New York: William Morrow, 1981.

American Psychological Association. "Unemployment and Mental Health." *APA Monitor*, Vol. 14, No. 1, 1983.

Anderson, Susan. "Starting Over: Life After Retirement." *The New York Times*, February 18, 1982, p. C1.

Araujo, Marianne. "Creative Nursing Administrator Sets Climate for Retention." *Hospitals*, May 1, 1980, pp. 72–76.

Arnold, John. *Shooting the Executive Rapids*. New York: McGraw-Hill, 1981.

Barron, James. "Humana Focus: Technology." *The New York Times*, August 14, 1984, p. D1.

Baruch, Grace; Rosalind Barnett; and Caryl Rivers. *Lifeprints*. New York: McGraw-Hill, 1983.

Becker, Ernest. *The Denial of Death*. New York: Free Press, 1973.

Behr, Marian, and Wendy Lazar. *Women Working Home*. Edison, N.J.: WWH Press, 1981.

Berg, Eric. "Shrinking a Staff the Kodak Way." *The New York Times*, September 4, 1983, p. F1.

Biracree, Tom. *How You Rate: Men*. New York: Dell, 1984.

Blair, Gwenda. "The Heart of the Matter." *Manhattan, Inc.*, October 1984, pp. 72–79.

Bleakley, John. "Citicorp's Atypical Leader." *The New York Times*, June 21, 1984, p. D1.

Bolles, Richard. *What Color Is Your Parachute?* Berkeley, Calif.: Ten Speed Press, 1984.

Bremer, Francis, and Emily Vogl. *Coping with His Success.* New York: Harper & Row, 1984.

Brenner, Harvey. *Mental Illness and the Economy.* Cambridge, Mass.: Harvard University Press, 1973.

Brody, Jane. "Workaholism." *The New York Times,* September 29, 1982, p. C1.

———. "Modifying 'Type A' Behavior Reduces Heart Attacks." *The New York Times,* August 7, 1984, p. C1.

Bureau of the Census. *Statistical Abstracts of the United States.* Washington, D.C.: U.S. Department of Commerce, 1982.

Butterfield, Fox. "Chinese Immigrant Emerges as Boston's Top Benefactor." *The New York Times,* May 5, 1984, p. A1.

Capon, Robert. "Being Let Go." *The New York Times Magazine,* August 5, 1984, p. 46.

Carter, Malcolm. "The Ins and Outs of Switching Jobs." *Money,* October 1981, pp. 124–28.

"Changing Schools: It Can Hurt." *The New York Times,* October 31, 1982, p. A78.

Cory, Christopher. "The Long-Lived Urge to Work." *Psychology Today,* September 1980, p. 21.

Cowles, Jerry. *How to Survive Getting Fired and Win!* New York: Warner Books, 1979.

Crystal, John, and Richard Bolles. *Where Do I Go from Here with My Life?* Berkeley, Calif.: Ten Speed Press, 1980.

Curtis, Charlotte. "The Dallas Billionaires." *The New York Times,* August 14, 1984, p. C12.

———. "A Tycoon with a New Bank." *The New York Times,* November 6, 1984, p. C12.

Deal, Terrence, and Allen Kennedy. *Corporate Cultures.* Reading, Mass.: Addison-Wesley, 1982.

Dessler, Gary. *Personnel Management.* Reston, Va.: Reston Publishing, 1981.

———. *Directory of Executive Recruiters.* Fitzwilliam, N.H.: Consultants News, 1982.

186

Bibliography

Drucker, Peter. "Thomas Watson's Principles of Modern Management." In *Esquire's Fifty Who Made the Difference*. New York: Villard Books, 1984.

Dun & Bradstreet. *Million Dollar Directory*. New York: Dun & Bradstreet, 1984.

Dunfee, Thomas. "Ethics and Productivity." *Wharton Alumni Magazine,* Winter 1984, pp. 37–42.

Erikson, Erik. *Identity and the Life Cycle*. New York: International University Press, 1959.

Farinelli, Jean. "What to Do if the Headhunter Doesn't Call." *MBA,* October/November 1978, pp. 30–34.

Feinberg, Mortimer. *Effective Psychology for Managers*. Englewood Cliffs, N.J.: Prentice-Hall, 1965.

Fitzpatrick, Jean Grasso. "The Dirty Truth About Housework." *Parents,* January 1984, pp. 51–55.

———. "Stop Working Late." *Working Woman,* October 1983, pp. 71–72.

Gardner, Judith. "In a Recession, Even Executives Takes Lumps." *U.S. News and World Report,* March 8, 1982, pp. 75–76.

Gettleman, Susan, and Janet Markowitz. *The Courage to Divorce*. New York: Simon and Schuster, 1974.

Gevirtz, Leslie. "You Need a Man Around the House." *The New York Post,* July 30, 1980, p. 5.

Goleman, Daniel. "Boss Seen as Best Buffer Against Stress." *The New York Times,* January 31, 1984, p. C1.

———. "As Sex Roles Change, Men Turn to Therapy to Cope with Stress." *The New York Times,* August 21, 1984, p. C1.

———. "Saying Goodbye Speaks Volumes." *The New York Times,* April 3, 1984, p. C1.

———. "Successful Executives Rely on Own Kind of Intelligence." *The New York Times,* July 31, 1984, p. C1.

Gould, Roger. *Transformations*. New York: Simon and Schuster, 1978.

"Have Talent, Will Travel." *U.S. News and World Report,* February 19, 1979, pp. 87–88.

Hayes, Thomas. "At Rolm, An Independent Style." *The New York Times,* September 27, 1984, p. D1.

Herzberg, Frederick. "One More Time: How Do You Motivate Employees?" *Harvard Business Review,* January/February 1968, pp. 53–62.

Hoffer, William. "Errers." *Success,* June 1984, pp. 21–23.

Holmes, Kay. "Working Wife and House Husband." *Parents,* February 1981, pp. 47–51.

Holmes, Thomas, and Richard Rahe. "The Social Readjustment Rating Scale." *Journal of Psychosomatic Research,* Vol. 11 (1967), pp. 213–18.

Horner, Matina, and Mary Walsh. "Psychological Barriers to Success in Women." In *Women and Success,* edited by Ruth Kundsin. New York: William Morrow, 1974.

Howe, Arthur. "Entrepreneurial Profiles." *American Way,* July 1984, pp. 51–55.

Howell, William, and Robert Dipboye. *Essentials of Industrial and Organizational Psychology.* Homewood, Ill.: Dorsey Press, 1982.

Johns, Gary. *Organizational Behavior.* Glenview, Ill.: Scott, Foresman and Co., 1983.

Jones, Landon. "The Mid-Career Switch." *Review,* September 1982, p. 28.

Kets De Vries, Manfred. "Unstable at the Top." *Psychology Today,* October 1984, pp. 26–34.

Kiechel, Walter. "When the Boss Is in Trouble." *Fortune,* March 1982, pp. 109–12.

Klemesrud, Judy. "Dr. Mathilde Krim: Focusing Attention on AIDS Research." *The New York Times,* November 3, 1984, p. B48.

———. "Special Relationship of Women and Their Mentors." *The New York Times,* April 11, 1984, p. A22.

Bibliography

Knowles, Daniel. "Stress Versatility and Uniqueness to Generate Interviews." *National Business Employment Weekly,* August 28, 1983, p. 7.

Krantzler, Mel. *Creative Divorce.* New York: M. Evans, 1973.

Kübler-Ross, Elisabeth. *On Death and Dying.* New York: Macmillan, 1969.

Lakein, Alan. *How to Get Control of Your Time and Your Life.* New York: Peter Wyden, 1973.

LaTour, Kathy. "What Motivates Mary Kay?" *American Way,* October 1984, pp. 154–58.

Leavitt, Harold. *Managerial Psychology.* Chicago: University of Chicago Press, 1964.

Levering, Robert; Milton Moskowitz; and Michael Katz. *The 100 Best Companies to Work for in America.* Reading, Mass.: Addison-Wesley, 1984.

Levinson, Daniel. *The Seasons of a Man's life.* New York: Alfred A. Knopf, 1978.

Lewin, Tamar. "Workers' Rights in a Closing Tested." *The New York Times,* July 19, 1984, p. D1.

Livingston, J. Sterling. "The Troubled Transition." *Journal of College Placement,* April/May 1970, pp. 1–7.

Machlowitz, Marilyn. *Workaholics.* Reading, Mass.: Addison-Wesley, 1980.

McCall, Jr., Morgan, and Michael Lombardo. "What Makes a Top Executive? *Psychology Today,* February 1983, pp. 26–31.

McDowell, Edwin. "Simon and Schuster's Empire Builder." *The New York Times,* November 11, 1984, p. F1.

Merwin, John. "Have You Got What It Takes?" *Review Magazine,* October 1981, pp. 31–37.

Millard, Max. "Isaac Asimov: West Side Workaholic." *The West Side,* November 10, 1977, p. 15.

Moldafsky, Annie. "How 'Power Widows' Feel About Success." *Success,* June 1984, pp. 12–15.

189

Mooney, Marta. "Does It Matter if His Wife Works?" *Personnel Administrator,* January 1981, pp. 43–49.

Morrison, Ann. "Job Hopping to the Top." *Fortune,* May 4, 1981, p. 127.

Mowday, R. T.; L. W. Porter; and R. M. Steers. *Employee-Organization Linkages.* New York: Academic Press, 1982.

Nathanson, Bruce. "Trapped in a Dead End Job?" *U.S. News and World Report,* June 1, 1981, p. 50.

National Commission on the Observance of International Women's Year. *To Form a More Perfect Union.* Washington, D.C.: U.S. Government Printing Office, 1976.

Nelson, Bryce. "How Does Power Affect the Powerful?" *The New York Times,* November 9, 1982, p. C1.

O'Brien, Mark. "Why They Leave." *Wharton Alumni Magazine,* Winter 1984, pp. 25–28.

Ouchi, William. *Theory Z.* Reading, Mass.: Addison-Wesley, 1981.

Paludi, Michele. "Horner Revisited: How Successful Must Anne and John Be Before Fear of Success Sets In?" *Psychological Reports,* Vol. 44, 1979, pp. 1319–22.

Peskin, Dean. *The Corporate Casino.* New York: AMACOM, 1978.

Peters, Thomas, and Robert Waterman. *In Search of Excellence.* New York: Warner Books, 1984.

"President Resigns at Bloomingdale's." *The New York Times,* April 11, 1984, p. D2.

Ray, Sr., Paul. "How Not to Get Fired." *Leaders,* Vol. 4 (1981), pp. 38–40.

Reif, Robin. "Breaking Up (With Your Job) Is Hard to Do." *Mademoiselle,* March 1984, p. 152.

Riegle, Donald. "The Psychological and Social Effects of Being Unemployed." *American Psychologist,* October 1982, pp. 1113–15.

Roche, Gerard. "Compensation and the Mobile Executive." *Harvard Business Review,* November/December 1975, pp. 53–57.

Bibliography

Roethlisberger, F. J., and W. J. Dickson. *Management and the Worker*. Cambridge, Mass.: Harvard University Press, 1939.

Rowan, Roy. "Rekindling Corporate Loyalty." *Fortune,* February 9, 1981, pp. 54–58.

Salmans, Sandra. "New Vogue: Company Culture." *The New York Times,* January 7, 1983, p. D1.

Schmidt, Warren, and Barry Posner. *Managerial Values and Perspectives*. New York: AMACOM, 1983.

Scott, Julia. "Women in the Work Force. *The New York Times,* November 11, 1982, p. C3.

Serrin, William. "Study Says Work Ethic Is Alive but Neglected." *The New York Times,* September 5, 1983, p. A8.

———. "Unions in Merck Strike Try to Involve the Public." *The New York Times,* August 18, 1984, p. A48.

Seybolt, John, and Duane Walker. "Attitude Survey Proves to Be a Powerful Tool for Reversing Turnover." *Hospitals,* May 1, 1980, pp. 77–80.

Shorris, Earl. *The Oppressed Middle*. New York: Anchor Press, 1981.

Siebert, Donald, and William Proctor. *The Ethical Executive*. New York: Cornerstone Library, 1984.

Simon, Robert. "What to Do if the Headhunter Calls." *MBA,* October/November 1978, pp. 20–30.

Smith, Joie. "Focus on Goals, Skills, and Accomplishments." *National Business Employment Weekly,* August 28, 1983, p. 7.

Solman, Paul, and Thomas Friedman. *Life and Death on the Corporate Battlefield*. New York: Simon and Schuster, 1983.

Sowell, Thomas. *Ethnic America*. New York: Basic Books, 1981.

Standard & Poor's. *Standard Corporation Descriptions*. New York: Standard & Poor's, 1985.

Straw, Barry. "Organizational Behavior." *Annual Review of Psychology,* Vol. 35 (1984), pp. 627–66.

Swartz, Herbert. "Restraining the Freedom to Change Jobs." *Citybusiness,* April 9, 1984, p. 27.

191

Bibliography

Thurow, Lester. "A Plague of Job Hoppers." *Time,* June 22, 1981, p. 66.

Triere, Lynette, and Richard Peacock. *Learning to Leave.* Chicago: Contemporary Books, 1982.

"U.S. Divorces Fell in '82; First Decline in 20 Years." *The New York Times,* March 16, 1983, p. A16.

Veiga, John. "Do Managers on the Move Get Anywhere?" *Harvard Business Review,* March/April 1981, pp. 1–9.

Waggoner, Walter. "James Brunot, 82, The First Producer of Scrabble Games." *The New York Times,* October 27, 1984, p. B33.

Wallis, Claudia. "Stress." *Time,* June 6, 1983, pp. 48–54.

Wareham, John. *Secrets of a Corporate Headhunter.* New York: Atheneum, 1980.

Wayne, Leslie. "The Method and Magic of the Superbroker." *The New York Times,* July 29, 1984, p. F1.

Weck, Thomas. *Moving Up Quickly.* New York: John Wiley, 1979.

Whyte, Jr., William. *The Organization Man.* New York: Simon and Schuster, 1956.

The World Almanac and Book of Facts. New York: Newspaper Enterprise Association, 1984.

Zonana, Victor. "The Porsches and Saabs at Schwab Aggravate Some at BankAmerica." *The Wall Street Journal,* January 20, 1983, p. 1.

Zucker, William. "Starting Your Own Business." *Wharton Alumni Magazine,* Winter 1984, pp. 18–21.

Index

Index

195

Index

197

Index

About the Author

DR. JACQUELINE HORNOR PLUMEZ holds a Ph.D. in psychology from Columbia University and a B.S. in Business Administration. She was an economist until she divorced that profession to become a psychologist. Dr. Plumez is the former president of the clinical division of the Westchester County Psychological Association and currently serves on its board of directors. She has written for *The New York Times Magazine, Working Woman,* and many other publications. Author of *Successful Adoption: A Guide to Finding a Child and Raising a Family,* she lives with her husband and two children.

KARLA DOUGHERTY earned her B.S. in journalism from the School of Public Communications at Boston University. A freelance writer, she has published works of both fiction and nonfiction, as well as many teleplays.